Richard Stewart and Donald Heyes

SCALE MODEL CANNON

HISTORY · DESIGN · CONSTRUCTION

JOHN MURRAY · LONDON

First published in Great Britain 1982 by
John Murray, Albemarle Street, London
All rights reserved
Unauthorized duplication contravenes
applicable laws

Typeset by Inforum Ltd, Portsmouth
Printed by Fletcher & Son, Norwich

British Library Cataloguing in Publication Data

Stewart, Richard
  Scale model cannon.
  1. Ordnance – Models
  I. Title   II. Heyes, Donald
  623.4′2′0228   UF527

  ISBN 0-7195-3888-2

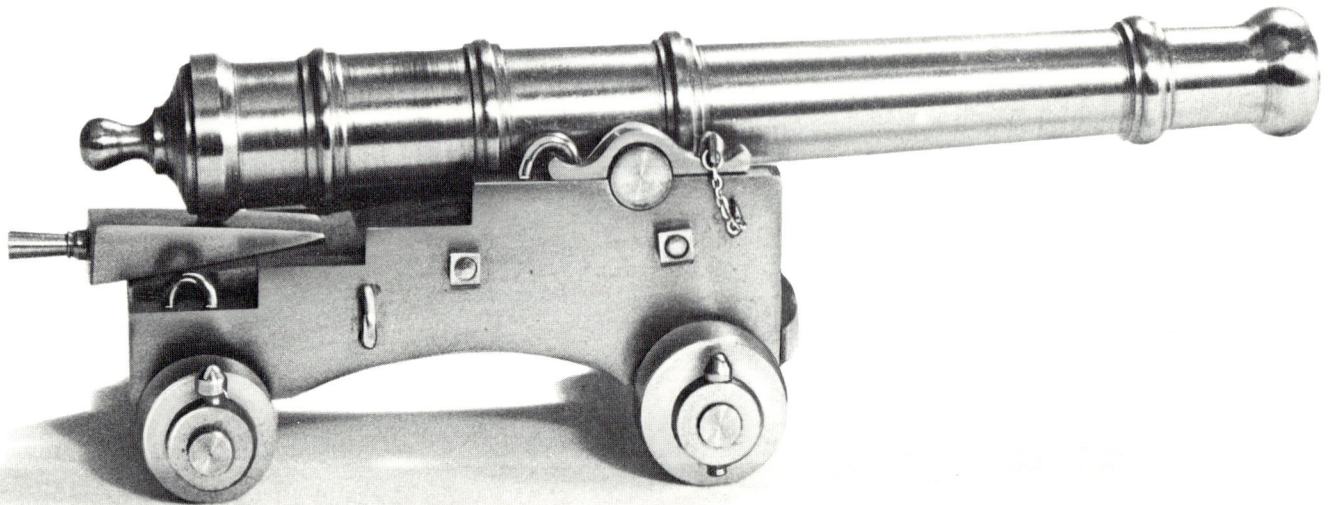

CONTENTS

INTRODUCTION

It is not known who first discovered gunpowder, although the Chinese probably used incendiary compounds in warfare before the Christian era began, and certainly used it for fireworks at an early date. In Europe the discovery has variously been attributed to two monks: Berthold Schwartz (who, it now appears, never existed!) and Roger Bacon who, in the thirteenth century, claimed that this magic substance would either blow your enemy up or put him to flight. Bacon was wise enough to conceal its dangerous formula in a cryptogram, but not long afterwards we find man's devious ingenuity had succeeded in exploiting gunpowder for projectile warfare and by the fourteenth century its use in Europe was widespread. For nigh on 600 years, smooth-bore muzzle-loaded ordnance came increasingly to dominate all forms of warfare on land and sea, inflicting gross damage on human beings and their property and profoundly affecting armour, fortifications, tactics and, indeed, the whole pattern of history.

Horrendous though the potential of real weapons might be, scale models are valued from the playroom to the boardroom, by schoolboys and generals alike, evoking an aesthetic response to polished metal and elegant design. For the model engineer they offer historical authenticity and an opportunity to exercise practical skill; for the school metalwork class they provide motivation, an introduction to varied workshop processes and an opportunity to read and prepare working drawings. The history of mechanical engineering, too, is closely linked: the cannon boring mills of the eighteenth century heralded a new range of industrial machines, with which many famous names such as Maudslay, Whitworth and Brunel were associated. Even Bessemer's famous converter was planned first and foremost to provide the necessary steel for gun making.

Our range of models covers the era of smooth-bore muzzle-loaders, each having been chosen for its visual appeal, historical significance and production feasibility in the amateur workshop. A compromise on some fine detailing has, of necessity, been reached, so that technical processes are within the scope of amateur and school. Thus all the models can be made with a small lathe such as the Myford ML7 and a small drilling machine or stand. The scale is economical in use of materials, yet sufficiently large for the beginner to achieve an acceptable degree of accuracy. Alternatively, the skilled amateur might wish to work to a more impressive scale of twice the size and add further detailing, while military modellers or war games enthusiasts might want to reduce it to one of their recognisable scales, particularly if a miniature lathe such as the Emco Unimat is available to them. Most of the materials used should be obtainable in their metric stock sizes but can be readily converted from their imperial equivalents.

One final point must be brought to the attention of the reader: these are not meant to be working models – no touch hole is included and the bore is only drilled out to sufficient depth to be mounted on a revolving centre in the lathe tailstock.

ACKNOWLEDGEMENTS

The authors are indebted to photographer Tony Hall and to the Rotunda Museum, Woolwich

GLOSSARY OF TERMS

(see also page 38 for cannon barrel details)

Artillery — Weapons of war that hurl projectiles by mechanical or explosive means, e.g. trebuchets, catapults and cannon; also that branch of the military service which uses these machines.

Barrel — Hollow tube of a firearm, named after the cooperage principle of manufacturing early wrought-iron pieces.

Bombard — Early large-bore ordnance (from the Greek *bombos*, meaning a noise).

Bore — Diameter of the inside of the barrel, or its internal length.

Breech — Rear section of the barrel – closed in muzzle-loaders or with an opening mechanism in breech-loaders.

Breeching rope — Heavy rope running from the breech of a ship's gun to the bulwarks to check recoil.

Button — Spherical knob cast on the cascable of the barrel to facilitate handling.

Cannon — Heavier pieces of ordnance as distinct from hand guns; originally not used to describe howitzers and mortars, but now associated with all smooth-bore muzzle-loading pieces.

Capsquare — Metal strap fitting over the barrel trunnion. It is secured by pins which pass through projecting pintles in the carriage sides, or by brackets.

Carriage — Wooden or metal frame for supporting the barrel – may have a double or single block trail.

Carronade — Short, thin-walled, iron cannon for firing large diameter shot over short ranges.

Cartridge — Pre-packed paper or cloth container holding a measured charge of gunpowder.

Cascable — End of barrel behind the breech, consisting of several mouldings tapering down to the knob.

Chase — That part of the barrel lying between the muzzle and the reinforce.

Dolphin — Lifting handle cast above the centre of gravity of smaller cannon, so called because of its resemblance to the animal.

Felloes — Six ash arcs dowelled together to form the rim of an artillery wheel.

Grape-Shot — Small pellets in a case for use as an artillery projectile.

Gun — Loosely applied to all artillery, but strictly speaking refers to long pieces of limited calibre for imparting high muzzle velocity.

Howitzer — Cross between a gun and a mortar, firing a heavier projectile on a curved trajectory and at a higher angle than the former, but being more mobile than the latter.

Knave	Central elm hub of an artillery wheel, morticed to receive twelve oak spokes.
Limber	Two-wheeled axle or carriage to which draught animals are harnessed and which is fixed onto the trail of the field guns to facilitate rapid movement.
Mortar	Short, heavy piece which fires large projectiles at a high angle, usually fixed at 45°.
Ordnance	General term to include all weapons of war, other than small-arms, which use an explosive charge to propel a missile.
Pintle	Plate which holds capsquare in position.
Quoin	Wooden wedge, forced under the breech, for elevating and depressing the barrel.
Reinforce	Thicker band of metal around the barrel.
Shell	Explosive artillery projectile.
Shot	Solid round projectile.
Trail	Double bracket or single block structure on a field carriage, running rearwards from the axletree down to the ground. Supports the barrel and absorbs recoil.
Trunnion	Pivot or gudgeon cast onto the barrel slightly in front of its balance point and below its centre line, by which it pivots on its carriage.
Windage	Gap between projectile and bore which allows propellant gases to escape, with consequent loss of power.

SELECTION OF MATERIALS

For the convenience of school metalwork classes and model engineers, the basic material chosen for the cannon is mild steel – that most useful and versatile of metals – which should be readily available to them. A bright drawn mild steel of good commercial quality is to be preferred, since it has an accurate finish, which facilitates marking out and polishing, particularly on flat and square-sectioned stock. For round sections, a free-cutting variety containing lead is easy to turn and produces a good finish on the barrels.

Alternatively, as indicated at appropriate places in the text, offcuts of hardwood such as mahogany and beech may be used to construct the carriages, and brass used for the barrels. Straight, close-grained pieces of timber should be selected, since these can be conveniently shaped with metalworking tools while a free cutting brass should be chosen for turning.

One inevitable problem with these metals is that steel will eventually rust and brass tarnish, especially after being handled.

This can be prevented by brushing with a proprietary metal lacquer (e.g. 'Ercalene' made by W. Canning & Co. Ltd., Great Hampton Street, Birmingham 18) or spraying with an aerosol lacquer obtained from a car accessory suppliers. Alternatively, steel barrels can be blackened to represent the original cast-iron by heating almost to red heat, and quenching off in sump oil. Hardwood parts may be given a variety of treatments ranging from stain and French polish to cellulose lacquer. A more subtle gloss is achieved by waxing over a coat of sealer, or by brushing with semi-matt polyurethane.

Most metal should be readily available, as listed in the preferred metric sizes for rounds, squares, flats and sheet. These are shown in the tables below, with their nearest imperial sizes alongside for the convenience of those still working in the latter. Naturally, the model engineer might not wish to stock the complete range of sizes, particularly of the rounds, but might obtain the principal ones and reduce them as appropriate.

Range of steel sections required to complete the models

Round		Square		Flats		Wire or Sheet		
mm	inches	mm	inches	mm	inches	mm	SWG	inches
6	$1/4$	6	$1/4$	6 × 32	$1/4 × 1^1/4$	1.2	18	$3/64$
8	$5/16$	10	$3/8$	6 × 40	$1/4 × 1^1/2$	1.6	16	$1/16$
10	$3/8$	12	$1/2$	8 × 32	$5/16 × 1^1/4$	2.0	14	$5/64$
12	$1/2$	16	$5/8$	8 × 40	$5/16 × 1^1/2$	3.0	10	$1/8$
16	$5/8$	18	$3/4$					
20	$3/4$							
25	1							
36	$1^3/8$							
40	$1^1/2$							

GUIDE TO THE TECHNICAL PROCESSES

Although specific instructions relating to each model are included in this book, together with working drawings, an introductory description is provided below of the basic processes involved. Because the barrels are the principal features these will be dealt with first and followed by notes on carriage construction and assembly.

Turning the barrels Ideally, in keeping with correct machine-shop practice, the barrels should be mounted and turned between centres so that they can be quickly and concentrically reversed for what is essentially two-setting work. However, for amateur purposes, two simpler procedures involving chuck work have been developed, one for the shorter mortars and one for the longer cannon. These allow for the major machining to be performed at one setting in the case of the cannon, and reversed only to complete the breech end of the mortars, on account of their larger diameters. (It should be noted that the addition of a three-jaw chuck and, ideally, a revolving centre to the basic lathe is necessitated, although this should present no problem to most school workshops. For greater accuracy and a more secure gripping action a four-jaw chuck could be used, despite the fact it takes longer to set up.)

Mortar barrels The mortar barrels firstly require a piece of round stock cut to a length approximately 2 mm over the final size. This is mounted in the three-jaw chuck, faced off, centre drilled (and pilot drilled for holes larger than 9 mm in diameter) and drilled out to the required diameter at the muzzle to receive a revolving centre. (If a revolving centre is not available, use a dead centre in the tailstock and only drill out the bore after all other turning has been completed. The large diameter bore may be beyond the drilling capacity of a small lathe, in which case drill to maximum possible size and enlarge further with a boring bar.)

The piece is now reversed in the chuck, faced off to length and (provided it is on centre height) the lathe tool used to scribe a diameter line across the face and a centre line down either side of what is to become the breech. (Of course, the fundamental difference between our method of model manufacture and that used for the original is that the barrel is not cast to its outer form with trunnions in place, but is turned from the solid and trunnions added afterwards.)

The next process is to mark out along this centre line and drill the trunnion hole at the breech end. Before starting to drill, ensure that the work is accurately centre punched and securely held in a machine vice, or clamped from the drilling machine bed into a vee block. Where the trunnions are at centre height drill right through, but where they lie below centre height, as in the case of the 8-inch brass mortar (and, indeed, all the longer cannon barrels), drill only to a depth of a few millimetres and then rotate the barrel several degrees so that the hole is off centre before drilling through. Remember that the chief danger in drilling occurs just when the point breaks through the underside, so special care should be taken to reduce the pressure on a sensitive feed machine.

Return the barrel to the lathe, gripping the breech end in the chuck and supporting the muzzle end on a revolving centre mounted in the tailstock. Now parallel turn it to the largest diameter, then progressively reduce to the smaller diameters between the reinforcing rings and, in the case of the 8-inch brass mortar, also taper turn the chase between the muzzle swell and the central reinforce. Finally, reverse the piece in the chuck with the breech end outwards and progressively round the breech, taking particular care over the trunnion hole. (As a somewhat easier alternative to drilling, a U-shaped hole may be filed into the breech to accept the trunnion. Provided that a reasonably tight fit is achieved, it can be fixed securely by soft soldering or with epoxy resin.)

Facing and centre drilling

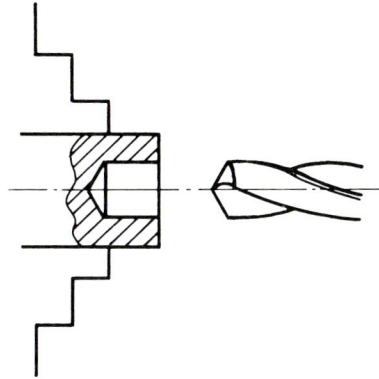

Drilling the bore

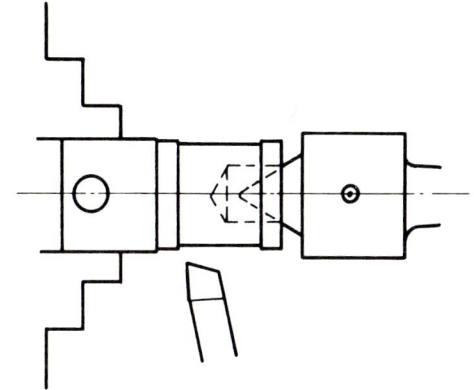

Parallel turning the mortar chase

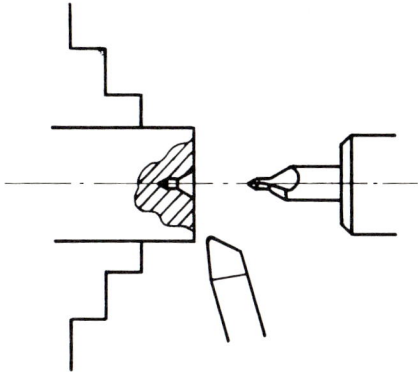

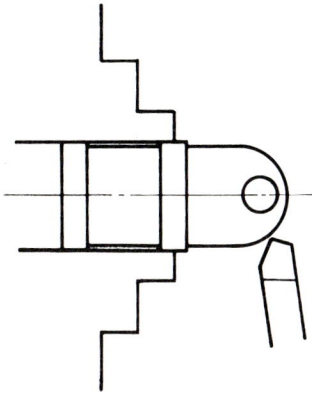

Rounding the mortar breech

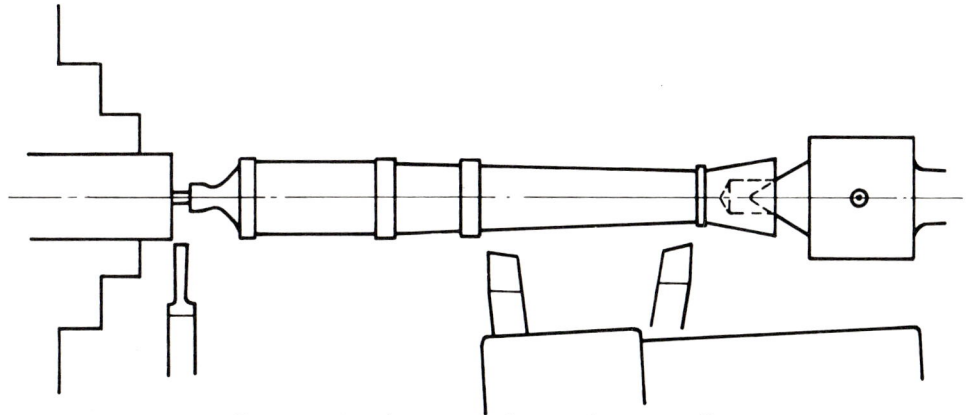

Taper turning the cannon chase and parting off

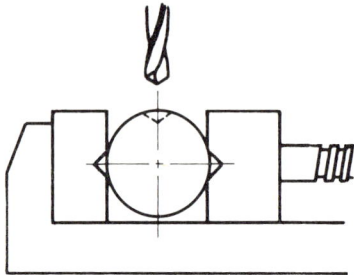

Drilling the trunnion hole

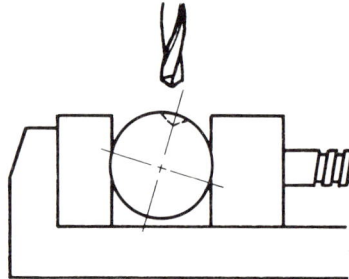

Drilling an offset trunnion hole after repositioning

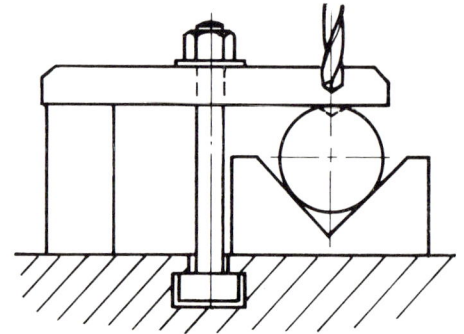

Alternative method of holding the barrel by bolting to the machine table

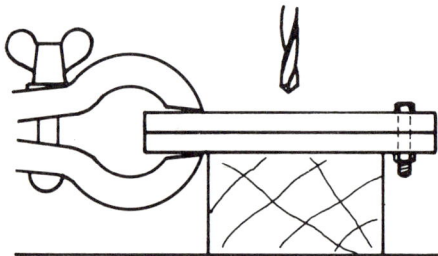

Drilling the carriage sides

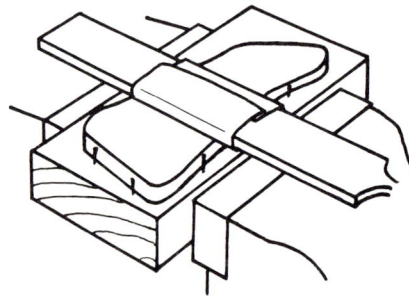

Holding and polishing a carriage side

press fit or epoxy resin

riveting

soft soldering

Joining the axles to the sides

Cannon Barrels   The majority of the lathework on the cannon barrels can be performed at one setting by mounting the barrel between the tailstock and three-jaw chuck. This requires that a piece of stock 20 mm or more longer than the final size be cut, most of surplus metal (the 'chucking piece') being placed in the chuck but leaving sufficient for parting off.

Firstly, however, the piece is faced off at its muzzle end, centre drilled and drilled out to the required bore diameter, as in the case of the mortars. Similarly, the trunnion hole has to be drilled through at this stage, although this feature is not required on the early swivel-mounted model or the carronade.

The principal turning can now take place. The surplus metal is gripped in the chuck and the breech mounted on a revolving centre in the tailstock. In effect, turning proceeds in a similar manner to that described for the mortar barrels, but the breech details can be turned in this one setting before the barrel is finally parted off. To avoid any danger, the last few millimetres could be hacksawed through and finished by filing to shape. In the case of the largest model, the ship's cannon, the chucking piece can be omitted and the breech end turned after being reversed in the chuck as with the mortars, although this does not give true concentricity to the button.

Constructing the carriages   Apart from the first model with its swivel mount, and the 8-inch mortar on its solid base, the carriages all have a fundamentally similar construction, being of two sides linked together by axles and bolts. The latter are fairly straightforward lathework exercises, involving parallel turning down to a shoulder, although a variety of techniques can be used to secure them in place and these, in turn, affect the tolerances involved.

The sides themselves are all made from 6 mm (or ¼-inch) flats. Marking out can be facilitated by first preparing an accurate template from card or, better still, sheet metal such as tinplate or aluminium, particularly if it is for a school metalwork class. To emphasise scribed lines, bright steel may be given a coat of copper sulphate solution or of a proprietary marking fluid. Light dot punching will further help definition when the sides are filed to shape, while axle holes will naturally require centre punching before they are drilled out.

In order to ensure that the sides are symmetrical, the following sequence should be adopted. Mark out the first side, centre punch and drill the axle and bolt holes. Position and clamp this over the second side and drill through one of the holes. A small nut and bolt or pin can now be used to assist further with alignment while the remaining holes are drilled. Separate the two sides and proceed with the outer shaping, removing the bulk of waste metal by hacksawing, drilling and chiselling. If a small vertical or horizontal milling machine is available this might usefully be employed, particularly for cutting any steps. To complete the shaping, clamp the two sides together in the vice and drawfile.

Finally a satin finish should be given to the flat surfaces by drawfiling them with a smooth file and then polishing them with emery cloth, or wet-and-dry paper, and oil. To hold irregularly shaped sides for this operation, pin them to a block of wood which in turn can be held in the vice.

Assembly   There are several ways of holding the carriages together. The simplest is to turn down the axles and bolts to ensure a push-fit assembly and coat the relevant surfaces with epoxy resin. A stronger joint can be made by soft soldering. However, this will require a chemical flux such as Baker's Fluid which must be fully washed away once the operation is completed. Further cleaning with emery cloth and oil will also be necessary to remove any surplus solder. Heating is best done with a small bottle-gas torch, or by gentle use of the brazing torch.

An alternative method is to turn the axles slightly over length and rivet them into their holes which have been countersunk. Naturally this will require further drawfiling and polishing of the outer surfaces. Perhaps for the skilled model engineer the most convenient answer is to turn the axles to press-fit tolerances and assemble using a press or engineer's vice.

Early swivel-mounted cannon, circa 1400

For many centuries, opposing armies had relied on three principal power sources in their war machines: the springiness of wood in giant crossbows, the elasticity of twisted ropes in torsion catapults and the counterbalancing pull of heaving weights in trebuchets. These could hurl massive darts, boulders, barrels of burning tar and even rotting corpses (an early form of germ warfare) at the unfortunate enemy. From the campaigns of Alexander the Great, around 300 BC, until Mohammed's siege of Constantinople in AD 1453, such contraptions remained essentially unchanged, although it is interesting to note that one development, the hand-held crossbow, had such a devastating effect on armoured knights that it was banned from 'civilised' warfare in 1139 as an 'atrocity'.

One can imagine, therefore, the dramatic effect in the fourteenth century of utilising the explosive force of gunpowder to fire a missile from a tube; only the cataclysmic potential of nuclear weapons 600 years later has conjured up greater horrors for mankind. Interestingly, like the crossbow, early ordnance fired arrows, although design quickly changed from a vase shape (*pot de fer* meaning 'firepot') to a more conventional barrel for firing iron or stone balls. Such barrels were either cast in bronze in the same way as church bells or, because of the difficulty of smelting large quantities of iron, were fabricated from wrought-iron bars encased with hoops on the cooperage principle – hence the name 'barrel'.

Unfortunately, wrought guns – often with a crude form of breech-loading – could be more dangerous to friend than enemy; King James II of Scotland, for example, was killed when his thigh bone was 'dung in two' by one exploding. Soldiers gave them a wide berth, while civilian gunners jealously guarded the secrets of their manufacture and operation. One German version, invented by Cotter, had its breech chamber secured by a heavy pin – the origin of today's term 'cotter pin'.

Despite the dangers and the limited technology, quite fantastic sizes were soon reached, particularly by the heavy siege guns: Mons Meg, now at Edinburgh Castle, has a wrought-iron barrel with a bore of $19\frac{1}{2}$ inches, while the bronze Dardanelles gun at the Tower of London has an enormous 25 inches, capable of firing a stone ball weighing 800 pounds. Indeed, the principal use of ordnance at this time was in siegework, defending or attacking castles and walled cities. The English are known to have first used guns to some effect at the siege of Calais in 1347, Edward III having assembled a train of artillery two years earlier for his invasion of France.

Our first model is a small, late fourteenth-century cannon, probably intended for defence of a fortification against attack. It has a wrought-iron barrel but, unlike larger weapons which lay on simple wooden blocks or carriages known as 'great trunks', it is strapped to a pivoted stock with an elevating quadrant and a swivel base. Prior to the invention of trunnions this was a means of mounting often used. For maximum effect against enemy personnel it could be loaded with scrap metal or nails known as 'langridge' which, in the following century, became known as 'cannister' or 'case' shot after the pre-packed containers used.

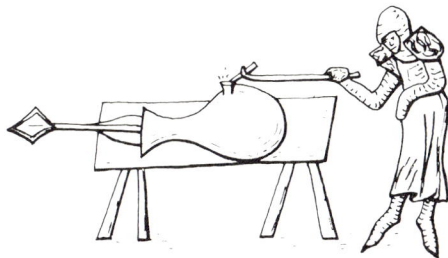

Pot de fer, 1326

CONSTRUCTION (SCALE 1:10)

Although the original barrel of such a cannon would have been fabricated from wrought-iron strips, the barrel of our first model, in keeping with all those to follow, is turned from bright mild steel. In contrast, the mounting for the cannon may be made from a suitably close-grained hardwood such as mahogany or beech. However, the cutting list and instructions do refer to mild steel. If wood is used instead, the cross-section of the quadrant arm could be increased slightly to 4 mm and reinforcing bands of thin sheet steel nailed around the pillar and base, as shown in the photograph on page 12.

Barrel   Mount a convenient length of 16 mm diameter rod (1) in the three-jaw chuck with approximately 35 mm protruding. Face off the end, centre drill and proceed to drill out the bore of the muzzle to a diameter of 8 mm and a depth of about 15 mm.

Now support the muzzle on a revolving centre mounted in the tailstock and parallel turn the length of the barrel to a diameter of 15 mm. Further reduce this to 14 mm between the three reinforcing bands so that they are left standing proud.

Finally part off at the breech end to give an overall length of 39 mm, withdrawing the revolving centre before making the final cut. Alternatively, hacksaw off the barrel and reverse and remount it in the chuck so that the breech can be faced off smooth.

Stock   Cut a 96 mm length of 10 mm square bar (2) and file the ends square to an overall length of 95 mm. Mark out a centre line down each side, using either spring dividers or a surface gauge, and centre punch for the pivot hole 30 mm from the front end. Holding the stock in a machine vice, drill out a 3 mm diameter hole.

Mark out the top and bottom tapers of the stock, either side of the centre lines, and file to shape. Now mark out a rear slot to fit around the curved quadrant arm, again using dividers or the surface gauge. Drill a 3 mm hole at the bottom of the slot and make two hacksaw cuts down to it to remove the bulk of the waste. Finally file the piece accurately to shape using small hand or needle files.

Pillar   Mount a 61 mm length of 18 mm square bar (5) in the four-jaw chuck and face off either end to a length of 60 mm. Now parallel turn down one end to a diameter of 8 mm for a length of 12 mm to fit into and swivel in the base. Remove from the lathe, mark out 4 mm x 45° chamfers front and rear, and file to shape.

At the opposite end mark out a 10 mm x 10 mm slot for the stock to pivot in. The majority of the waste can be removed by drilling out a hole, 10 mm in diameter, before hacksawing and filing out the remainder with a square file. Mark out and shape two chamfers to match those at the lower end. Next, mark out and centre punch an elevation pin hole 3 mm from the top and, holding the work in a machine vice, drill out to a diameter of 3 mm through both sides.

Finally, mark out and drill two 3 mm diameter holes near the base of the pillar to take the quadrant arm spigots.

Frame or quadrant arm   The elevation quadrant is shaped from two pieces of 3 mm strip (3). Use a card or aluminium template to mark out a curved quadrant on a piece of 56 mm x 15 mm x 3 mm strip. Centre punch six 3 mm diameter holes and, holding the work firmly in the machine vice, carefully drill them out. Hacksaw off the waste metal and file the outer contours to shape. Finally, file carefully around the lower end to create two 3 mm diameter spigots to slot into the horizontal part of the arm.

The horizontal is marked out on a piece of 5 mm x 15 mm x 3 mm strip (4). Centre punch and drill two 3 mm diameter holes for the spigots which have been filed into the curved quadrant. File the taper on either side for its full length and then file two

EARLY SWIVEL-MOUNTED CANNON

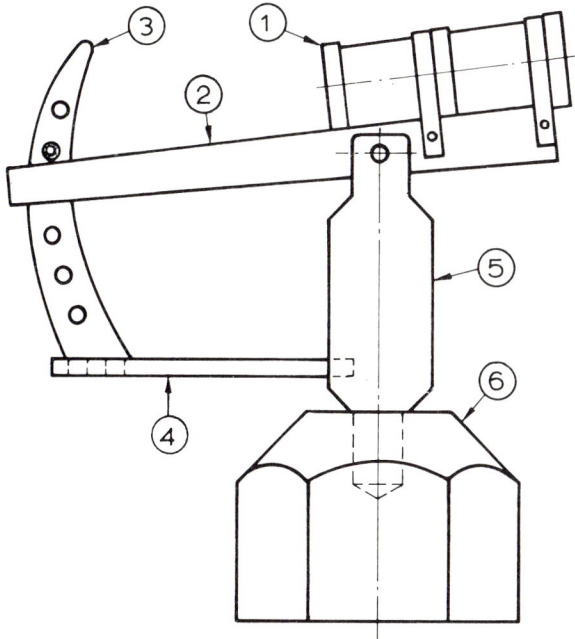

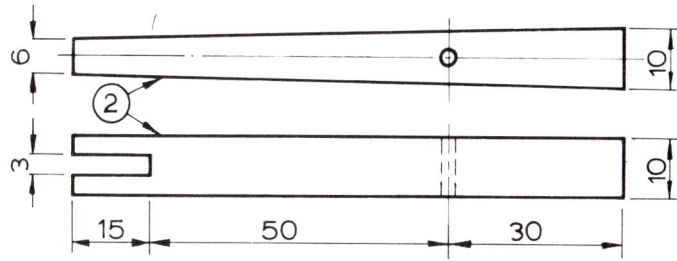

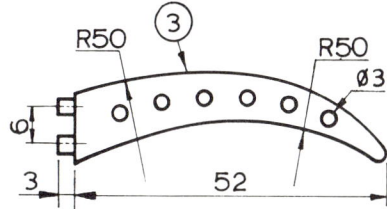

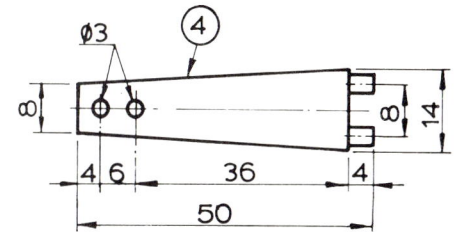

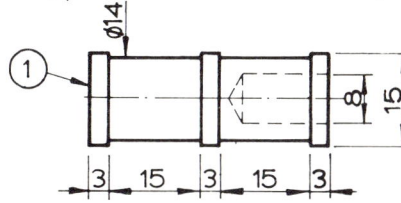

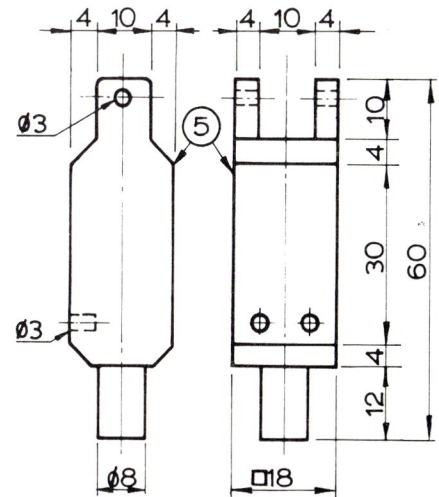

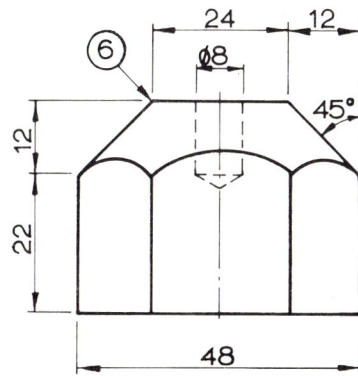

ITEM	NAME	NO.	CUTTING SIZE
1	BARREL	1	16 DIA. ROD
2	STOCK	2	96 x 10 SQUARE
3	FRAME	1	56 x 15 x 3 STRIP
4	FRAME	1	51 x 15 x 3 STRIP
5	PILLAR	1	61 x 18 SQUARE
6	BASE	1	35 x 41 A/F

SCALE 4:5

15

spigots on this piece to fit accurately into the pair of holes in the base of the pillar.

Base   This is turned from a 35 mm length of 41 mm across-flats hexagonal stock (6). Mount in the three-jaw chuck and face off one end to create the underside. Reverse the piece in the chuck and face off the opposite end, the top, thereby reducing the finished length to 34 mm. Now set the compound slide to an angle of 45° and turn a 12 mm chamfer at the top corner. Finally, centre drill and drill out an 8 mm diameter hole to a depth of 18 mm, to accommodate the circular base of the pillar.

Assembly   Polish each part with emery cloth and coat all exposed surfaces with lacquer. If hardwood has been used for the mounting, finish this piece with fine glasspaper and polish with semi-matt polyurethane or wax.

Fasten the barrel to its stock by means of two thin steel straps, which should be bent to shape and then riveted in place with two 1.6 mm pins fitting into two holes, of appropriate size, drilled in the stock. Tinplate, polished down to the bare steel with an emery cloth, is a useful source of thin sheet metal for the amateur engineer, and panel pins cut to length make convenient rivets.

Coat the spigots of the curved quadrant sparingly with epoxy resin and fit them into the horizontal arm. It is possible to make a stronger joint by riveting over the two spigots or by soft soldering the pieces together. The arm should now be placed in the pillar and fixed with epoxy resin or by soft soldering.

Position the stock across the top of the pillar and fix it in position with a 3 mm pin which is itself held in place by epoxy resin or by light riveting. Finally pass a taper pin through the curved quadrant to hold the stock at any one of the six elevating positions, and mount the pillar in the base.

Elizabethan culverin, circa 1575

The individuality of early guns, such as Mons Meg, made stan-dardisation difficult – a problem not unknown to modern armies! Pieces were often named after saints or famous people, but a variety of exotic titles appeared in the Middle Ages based on birds of prey, reptiles or strange and mythical beasts: for example, siren, falcon, pelican and dragon. The term 'culverin' (meaning snake or snake-like) denoted a long-barrelled and consequently long-range gun, lying midway between the large 'cannons' and small 'falconets'.

When suitably mounted, these cumbersome weapons were just manoeuvrable enough for tactical application on the battlefield, and history records the French as using them by 1450. At the Battle of Formigny in that year, two culverins inflicted serious casualties on the English who were attempting to retain their French territories. However, for the next century, siege warfare remained artillery's principal role. It often terrorised defenders into surrender without a single shot being fired. Even the towering walls of Constantinople, Christendom's last Eastern fortress

Sixteenth-century culverin and cannoneer

against the Turks, were finally breached when Mohammed had constructed a gun so large that its explosion was said to cause miscarriages in pregnant women twelve miles away. But because of the atrocious state of the roads, field guns often arrived too late to influence fighting on the battlefield. Eventually, by 1512, at the Battle of Ravenna, concentrated fire by French artillery led to a decisive defeat of the Spanish – although, in return, a Spanish cannon ball is claimed to have knocked down forty men.

Not until 1547, at the coastal battle of Pinkie, near Inveresk, did the English use field artillery decisively, and here they were able to fire on the unfortunate Scots from both land and sea. Many of these early guns used by the English were either pur-chased or captured abroad. Indeed, we had been regarded as a somewhat backward nation before the reign of Henry VIII, who established a small permanent artillery and an armaments indus-try to supply it. First bronze and then iron guns were successfully cast in the Weald of Sussex under the supervision of iron master Ralph Hogge. Thereafter Wealden craftsmen became most skil-led, achieving optimum proportions and weight in functionally efficient designs while their continental rivals were still fancifully decorating not only guns, but also cannon balls. As is so often the case, man's aggressive instincts contributed to political and economic growth, and Gentilini, Italy's most famous gun-founder, was prompted to write: 'English are judicious people and of great intelligence . . . and are very ingenious in their inven-tions.'

During Elizabethan times, the old wrought-iron barrels were increasingly replaced by cast ones and rationalised into three main categories: cannon, culverins and mortars, or their various sub-divisions. Cannon remained essentially large calibre wall-breakers while the lighter culverins were more appropriate to the battlefield. Barrels, which had previously been quite literally

carted about, were mounted directly on two-wheeled gun carriages with double trails for supporting the weight and the shock of firing. Trunnions, cast integrally with the barrel, enabled it to swing directly on the trail cheeks. Axle and transoms connected the two trails and a wedge driven between bed and breech facilitated elevation. The axle tips were linked to the trails with iron stays in an attempt to absorb the thrust of recoil, and the wooden carriage and wheels were substantially reinforced all over with iron straps and bolts.

For the Navy, carriage design was inevitably simpler, the ships themselves providing manoeuvrability. Yet culverins had their greatest success when the English out-gunned the Spanish Armada in 1588 using long-range, medium-shotted culverins against short-range, heavy-shotted cannon.

CONSTRUCTION (SCALE 1:20)

The carriage and wheels of the culverin may be made from hardwood, suitably reinforced with thin steel bands as shown in the photograph, or, alternatively, made from mild steel throughout. The cutting list and text refer to the latter. Because this is a fairly complex model, beginners may wish to tackle it after first making the light 3-pounder, although many of the intricate fittings can be simplified, or even omitted.

Barrel Mount a convenient length (minimum 135 mm) of 16 mm diameter rod (1) well into the three-jaw chuck. Face off the end, centre drill, and drill out the bore to a diameter of 4 mm and a depth of 15 mm.

Remove the piece from the lathe, centre punch 66 mm from the muzzle end for the trunnion hole and, holding the piece in a machine vice, drill a 4 mm diameter hole to a depth of 3 mm. Now, reposition the work so that the hole is off centre and drill right through.

Remount the piece in the chuck with approximately 130 mm protruding and the muzzle end supported on a revolving centre. Set the top-slide to an angle of 1° and taper turn the barrel to the dimensions shown, leaving the reinforcing bands in relief. Carefully form these with an appropriately ground tool, reduce the metal around the cascable, and similarly finish the bands. Leave approximately 3 mm in diameter still securing the button to the parent metal in the chuck before finally hacksawing through and finishing the button to a smooth curve with a file.

The trunnion (2) is made from 6 mm diameter rod turned down to 4 mm and faced off to a length of 28 mm. Alternatively, if 4 mm diameter stock is available this may be used and simply faced off at either end.

Trails Mark out the two trails (3) on 150 mm x 16 mm x 6 mm strips. Scribe a centre line around each using a surface gauge or spring dividers, and step off the centres of the four 3 mm holes. Mark out the outer contours of each trail, starting with an 8 mm semi-circle at the fore end. A sheet-metal template may be used to assist marking out.

Centre punch and drill out four holes in one of the sides. Now use this as a guide to drill out the second side (after the first hole has been drilled, a length of 3 mm diameter rod may be slipped down the holes to maintain alignment). Shape the outer contours of each side separately, by hacksawing and filing, then clamp the two together again in the vice and complete by drawfiling. The trunnion groove should be formed with a round file or, alternatively, drilled while the two trails are clamped edge to edge.

Transoms The three transoms are made from the same section material as the trails. Saw off a 24 mm length of the 16 mm x

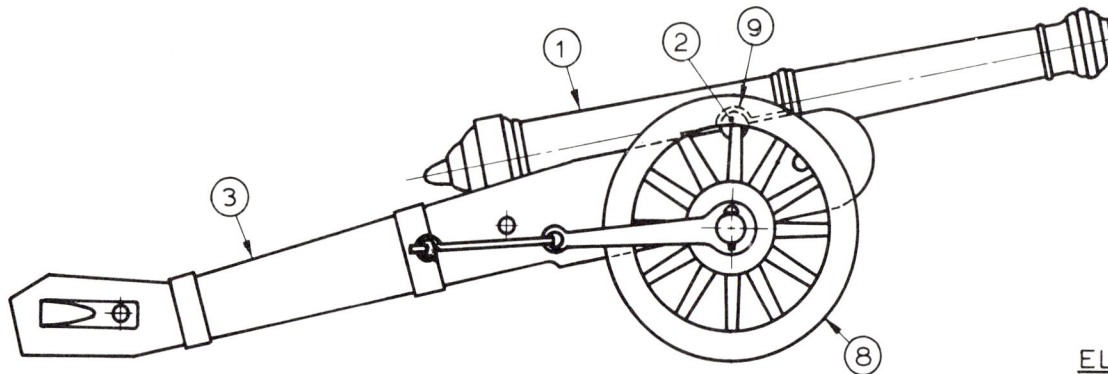

ELIZABETHAN CULVERIN

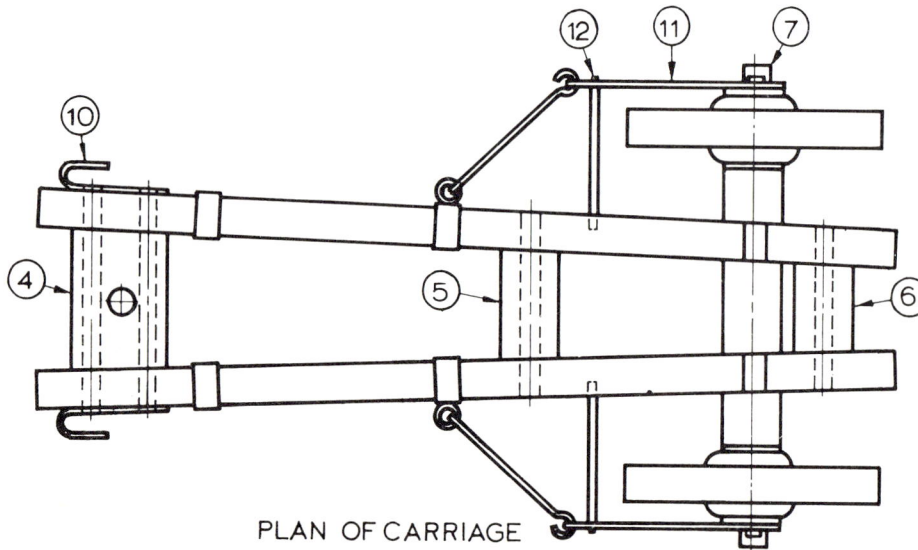

PLAN OF CARRIAGE

SCALE 4:5

ITEM	NAME	NO.	CUTTING SIZE
1	BARREL	1	16 DIA. ROD
2	TRUNNION	1	6 DIA. ROD
3	TRAIL	2	150 x 16 x 6 STRIP
4	REAR TRANSOM	1	24 x 16 x 6 STRIP
5	MID TRANSOM	1	19 x 11 x 6
6	FORE TRANSOM	1	16 x 11 x 6
7	AXLETREE	1	80 x 10 SQUARE
8	WHEEL	2	45 DIA. ROD
9	CAPSQUARE	2	27 x 7 x 1 SHEET
10	HAULING HOOK	2	30 x 6 x 1 SHEET
11	RECOIL STAY	2	42 x 11 x 1 SHEET
12	STRUT	2	27 x 1·6 DIA. WIRE

20

6 mm strip for the rear transom (4). Mark out on one of the end faces two 3 mm diameter holes, centre punch and drill through the full length, ensuring that the work is held absolutely vertical in the machine vice. Now mark out and drill the 4 mm diameter 'trail eye' in the centre of the transom.

There is a slight taper on each transom to fit between the trails. On the rear transom this amounts to a reduction from 23 mm to 22 mm as shown in the drawing, and this should be achieved by accurate marking out and filing.

The middle transom (5) is shaped from a piece of strip sawn to 19 mm x 11 mm x 6 mm. File to a width of 10 mm and mark out and drill a single 3 mm diameter hole through it. Now file the ends to size with the necessary taper from 18 to 17.5 mm.

Saw off an 11 mm wide piece of 16 mm x 6 mm strip for the fore transom (6) and file down to 10 mm. Mark out and drill a 3 mm diameter hole and complete by filing the tapers from 14.5 to 14 mm. While the carriage is being assembled, some slight adjustment may have to be made to these tapers to ensure an accurate fit.

Axletree This may be made in one of two ways; either by turning the two axles from the piece of square steel that has been used for the axle beam or, alternatively, by inserting two pieces of rod into the beam. If you are using the former method, mount an 80 mm x 10 mm square length (7) in the four-jaw chuck with 20 mm protruding. Face it off, and reduce it to a 5 mm diameter for 16 mm. Mark out the 48 mm length of the beam, reverse the piece in the chuck, and turn the axle at the opposite end. An angle of 5° must be introduced between the axles and the beam. This can be accomplished by tapping with a hammer, cushioning the metal with a block of hardwood.

A more satisfactory method of achieving the angle is to face off a length of 8 mm square bar to 48 mm and drill two 5 mm diameter holes in the ends at the required 5°. Drill the holes to a depth of 6 mm to accommodate two axles, 16 mm long and 5 mm in diameter.

Wheels Although the original wheels were built up from separate spokes and felloes in the manner used for carts – and, indeed, the one used for the photographed model – it is easier to turn them from the solid and cut out the spaces between the spokes.

Mount a length of 45 mm round stock (8) in the three-jaw, or preferably four-jaw, chuck with approximately 25 mm protruding. Face off, centre drill and drill out a 5 mm axle hole to a depth of 20 mm. Now, reduce the diameter to 15 mm for a length of 3 mm to form the knave, and undercut between the outer rim and the knave to define the position of the spokes, rounding off the knave as shown in the drawing.

The inner face of the wheel can now be partly formed by taking a broad cut with the parting tool, leaving a rim width of 6 mm and then parting off the knave to a width of 12 mm. Alternatively, the wheel can be cut off in the power hacksaw, or a combination of parting and hacksawing may be used.

Remount the wheel in the four-jaw chuck with the inner face outwards, ensuring that it is absolutely on centre. Proceed to undercut between the rim and the knave, and complete by rounding off the knave. It is also possible to carry out these turning operations by mounting the piece on a taper mandril between centres.

Remove the wheel from the lathe and scribe on it the positions of the twelve spokes. Carefully mark the centres for twelve holes, 4 mm in diameter, to remove the bulk of waste between them and drill out. A further twelve 2 mm diameter holes may be drilled out nearer the knave before the removal of waste and the shaping of the spokes with needle files is completed.

Capsquare Cut a 27 mm x 7 mm strip of 1 mm sheet (9) using a junior hacksaw or tinsnips, and file square to a finished size of 26.5 mm x 6 mm. Mark out and cut the two 5 x 1 mm pintle slots, by drilling a line of 1 mm holes and finishing with a needle file. Finally, form a 4 mm diameter curve to slot over the trunnion by punching into a creasing iron, or into a groove cut into a block of hardwood.

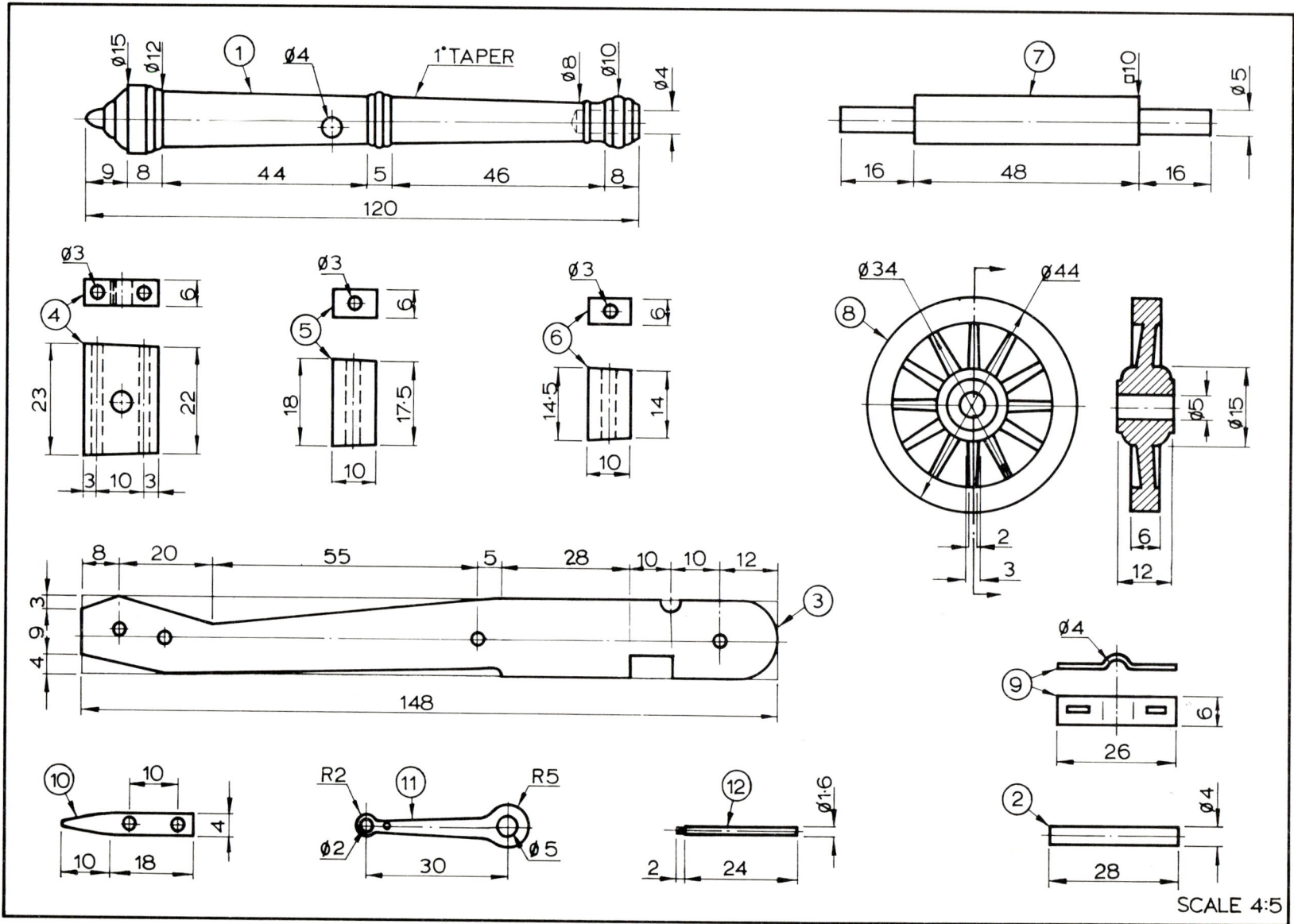

Ø15
Ø12
① Ø4
1°TAPER
Ø8
Ø10
Ø4

9 8 44 5 46 8
120

⑦
Ø10
Ø5

16 48 16

Ø3
④
Ø3
⑤
Ø3
⑥

6 6 6

23 22
18 17·5
14·5 14

3 10 3
10
10

⑧ Ø34 Ø44
Ø5 Ø15

2
3
6
12

8 20 55 5 28 10 10 12
③
3
9
4 9

148

⑩
10
4
10 18

R2 ⑪ R5
Ø2 30 Ø5

⑫ Ø1·6
2 24

Ø4
⑨
26
6

② Ø4
28

SCALE 4:5

22

The pintles and pins can be appropriately shaped from offcuts of 1 mm sheet or, alternatively, the capsquares simply held in position with plain pins.

Fittings The hauling hooks (10) and recoil stays (11) are also shaped from 1 mm sheet and are drilled and filed to the dimensions shown. During drilling, the small pieces of metal should be held securely in a hand vice on a block of wood. The recoil stays rest against struts (12). These have small shoulders which are turned or filed at their outer ends, and are linked to the trails by wire hooks, bent to shape from 1 mm diameter wire with round-nosed pliers.

The transom bolts can be cut from 3 mm diameter wire or welding rod, and the various metal reinforcing strips cut from tin plate emery clothed down to the bare steel.

Assembly Polish each part carefully with emery cloth, and coat all exposed surfaces with lacquer. If hardwood has been used for the carriage and wheels, finish with fine glass paper and polish with semi-matt polyurethane or wax.

Assemble the carriage by slotting four 3 mm diameter tie rods through the sides and transoms and then slot the axletree in position. Because of the taper, final adjustment to the angles with smooth files may be necessary to ensure the best fit, as noted earlier. All these parts may be held permanently together by the sparing use of epoxy resin or by soft soldering. Alternatively, the tie rods can be cut slightly longer and riveted over. This is a particularly appropriate method for the rear transom rods which pass through the hauling hooks. The hauling hooks themselves should be curved to shape with round-nosed pliers after assembly.

The reinforcing straps on the carriage and wheels can be bent to shape, sparingly coated with epoxy resin, and held in position with pins and rubber bands until the adhesive is set.

Now slot the wheels into position, assemble the recoil stays and drop the axle pins into place. Finally, glue the trunnion in position and fix the barrel to the carriage with the capsquare and pins.

Light 6-pounder, circa 1750

Titles such as 'falconet', 'drake' and 'dragon' originally denoted guns lighter than culverins, but by 1700 the term 'cannon', formerly reserved for heavy siege guns, was adopted throughout. Classification was now by shot weight, or, in the case of mortars, by calibre, popular sizes being 3, 6, 12, 18, 24 and 32 pounds and 8, 10 and 13 inches.

Essential features of barrel design changed little over a period of 300 years, and are evident in our light 6-pounder, with its progressive taper towards muzzle swell and staged reinforcing bands. Trunnions and dolphins were included in the casting, as this facilitated adjustment and handling. In addition, the breech knob could hold a sling, which was secured at its other end to a handspike inserted down the bore. For small guns, bronze was preferred to iron since, although it was more expensive, it weathered well and was extremely tough, making possible lighter, thinner walls. It even gave some forewarning of explosion by bulging slightly beforehand. Lack of metallurgical knowledge meant that rule-of-thumb formulae were used in casting: for example, 225 lb of gunmetal for each pound of projectile weight.

6-pounder field gun with five-man crew

As a safeguard, no gun was considered acceptable until it had been 'proved' with a large charge of powder.

In the early days, small guns were carried about in 'petits charrois', a form of wheelbarrow. The commander who first exploited guns as mobile weapons was King Gustavus Adolphus of Sweden, the 'father of modern warfare'. During his Polish campaigns of the 1620s he even used *kalter* (leather) guns weighing as little as 90 lb. These consisted of copper tubes bound with hemp or wire and enveloped in leather. (This anticipated in concept a method of construction used in modern weapons.) However, the more reliable light cast guns could still be handled by two men and drawn by one horse. A fast-moving version, as its name implies, was the 'galloper' gun with twin shafts for the single horse.

Another monarch, Frederick the Great of Prussia, set standards of training and organisation for mobile artillery which came to be adopted throughout Europe in the eighteenth century. In particular, he introduced horse artillery, made possible by the adoption of the limber — a separate two-wheeled axle, hooked under the trail to permit rapid harnessing. Eventually, the development of the single block trail, which elevated screw and limber, led to horse artillery becoming an integral part of the British Army in 1793, with 6-pounders being their principal weapons, as they were to the Prussians.

Our chosen model is based on a bronze barrel, cast in 1752 as a field gun. For ceremonial purposes it was remounted on an iron carriage in 1886, and today peacefully guards a war memorial. Such is its simplicity and elegance that it offers a fitting choice for the model-maker. However, on their original lightweight wooden field-carriages, particularly after the introduction of the block trail in 1792, the 6-pounders saw more campaign action than any other British gun. One was even hauled up the Heights of

Abraham for the capture of Quebec in 1754. Napoleon himself regretted that the French had been virtually the only European nation not to adopt 6-pounders, and justified replacing their 4- and 8-pounders on the grounds that his officers could never decide which to use. More importantly, his Grand Army could now exploit captured 6-pounder ammunition.

When firing against infantry, the barrel was elevated between 0° (point blank) and 4° to produce 'ricochet' fire in which the shot bounced murderously along the ground. At 4° elevation, 1½ lb of gunpowder achieved a range of 1200 yards; greater elevations and distances only led to a fall off in velocity and to solid shot burying itself harmlessly in the earth. At such distances, anyway, one could hardly see the enemy let alone the results. Similarly,

guns were not to be sited on too high a hill nor fired over the heads of attacking soldiers, who might duck and break their stride!

Numerous small cannon such as the 6-pounder would also be found guarding fortification walls and on upper decks of ships, mounted on garrison standing carriages rather like the one the model stands on. These carriages were made of oak or elm, with cast-iron wheels on land and elm wheels at sea to protect the decks. Many fortification carriages were made entirely of iron, as it was more durable in coastal sea air or in the tropics, but because it shattered dangerously under fire a spare wooden carriage had to be stored for wartime use. Eventually, most wooden carriages rotted away and those which remain in museums or on display have been rebuilt.

CONSTRUCTION (SCALE 1:15)

The barrel of the photographed model has been turned from mild steel, but for a more authentic appearance the reader might wish to substitute brass and finish the carriage in a contrasting black.

Barrel Mount a convenient length (minimum 115 mm) of 15 mm diameter rod (1) well into the three-jaw chuck. Face off the end, centre drill and drill out the bore to a diameter of 6 mm and a depth of 10 mm.

Remove the piece from the lathe, centre punch 60 mm from the muzzle end for the trunnion hole and, holding it in a machine vice, drill a 5 mm diameter hole to a depth of 3 mm. Now reposition the work so that the hole is off centre, and drill right through.

Remount the piece in the chuck with approximately 105 mm protruding and the muzzle end supported on a revolving centre. Set the top-slide to an angle of 2° and taper turn the barrel to the dimensions shown, leaving the reinforcing bands in relief. Now reduce and shape the metal around the cascable leaving a length, approximately 3 mm in diameter, securing the button to the

parent metal held in the chuck. Finally, hacksaw carefully through this and file the button to a smooth curve.

The trunnion (2) is made from 6 mm diameter rod turned down to 4 mm and faced off to a length of 30 mm. If dolphins are added they can be bent to shape from 30 mm lengths of 1.6 mm diameter steel or brass wire to fit into four holes drilled just within the central reinforcing bands, as shown in the photograph.

Carriage sides Mark out the two carriage sides (7) on 86 mm x 40 mm x 6 mm strips using a card or sheet metal template. Centre punch and drill out the five 3 mm tie rod/bed bolt holes and a 5 mm axletree hole in one of the sides. Now use this as a guide to drill out the second side. Hacksaw off the waste metal and file each side to shape using a half-round file for the hollow curves and a round file for the trunnion groove. During drilling and filing short pins of 3 mm welding rod, placed in the holes already drilled, can be used to keep the two sides in place and thus ensure symmetry.

LIGHT 6-POUNDER

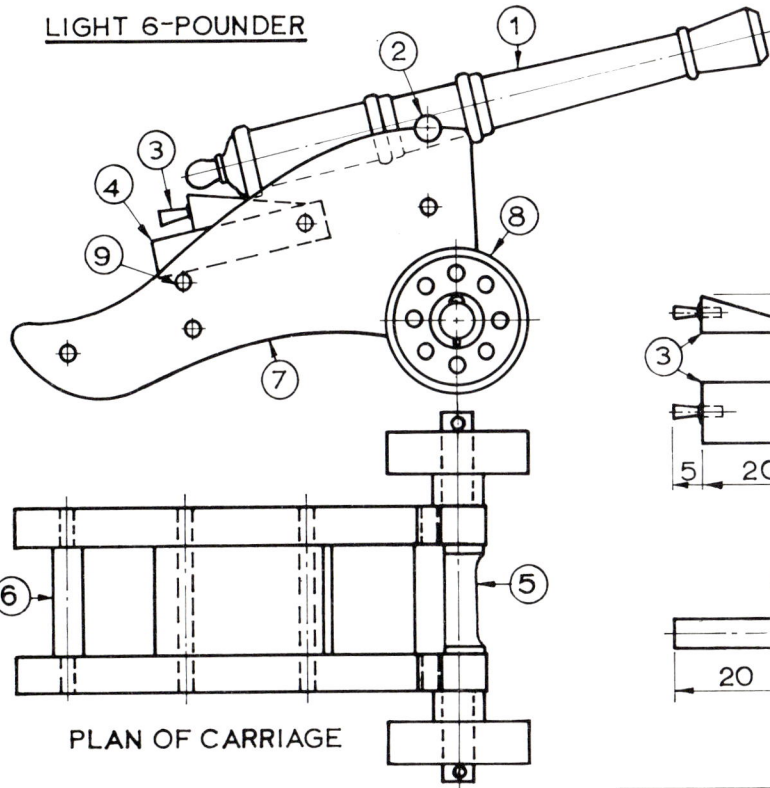

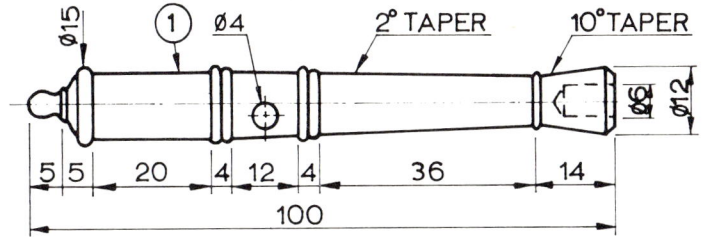

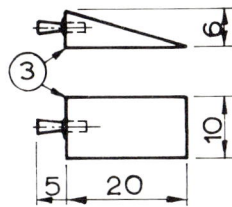

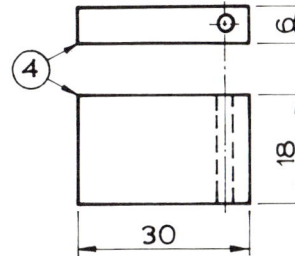

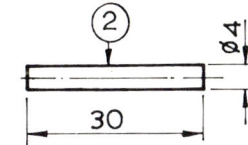

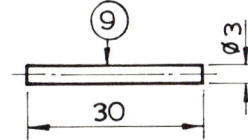

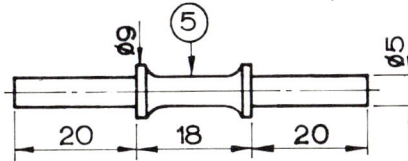

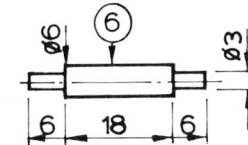

PLAN OF CARRIAGE

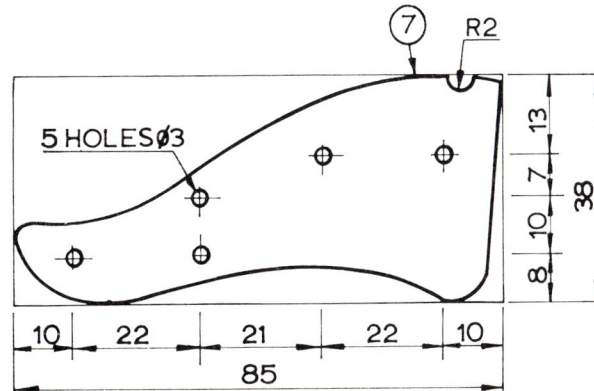

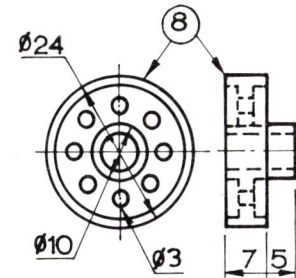

Ø15 ① Ø4 2° TAPER 10° TAPER

5 5 20 4 12 4 36 14
100

③ 5 20

④ 30

② Ø4 30

⑨ Ø3 30

Ø9 ⑤ Ø5
20 18 20

Ø6 ⑥ Ø3
6 18 6

⑦ R2
5 HOLES Ø3
13 7 10 8 38
10 22 21 22 10
85

Ø24 ⑧
Ø10 Ø3 7 5

ITEM	NAME	NO.	CUTTING SIZE
1	BARREL	1	16 DIA. ROD
2	TRUNNION	1	32 x 6 DIA. ROD
3	WEDGE	1	22 x 11 x 6
4	PLATFORM	1	32 x 20 x 6
5	AXLETREE	1	60 x 10 DIA. ROD
6	TIE ROD	3	32 x 6 DIA. ROD
7	SIDE	2	86 x 40 x 6 STRIP
8	WHEEL	2	25 DIA. ROD

SCALE 4:5

Axletree   The axletree (5) is turned from a 60 mm length of 10 mm diameter rod. Face off each end to an overall length of 58 mm, position the piece in the chuck with 22 mm protruding and turn down to a diameter of 5 mm for a length of 20 mm. Reverse the work in the chuck and similarly reduce the other end to 5 mm in diameter. Reposition in the chuck with the middle section exposed and reduce this first to 9 mm in diameter and then to 5 mm in diameter, as shown in the diagram. Alternatively, the axletree may be turned between centres to avoid flexing, a slightly longer piece of stock being used from which the centre holes are later faced off. Finally, drill a 1.6 mm hole through either end to accept the wheel pins (though these are not required if the wheels are to be held in place by riveting over the axletree ends).

Tie rods and bed bolts   The three tie rods (6) are each made from 32 mm lengths of 6 mm diameter rod, faced off to a length of 30 mm and reduced to 3 mm in diameter for a length of 6 mm at either end to go in the carriage sides.

Either 3 mm diameter wire or welding rod can be used for the two bed bolts (9). These are also finished to lengths of 30 mm, by filing or facing off in the lathe.

Platform   The platform or bed (4) is shaped from a 32 mm x 20 mm x 6 mm strip. Alternatively, with careful sawing, a suitably sized off-cut can be obtained from one of the carriage sides. File both ends square to an overall length of 30 mm, centre punch 4 mm from one end and drill out a hole, 3 mm in diameter, for the front bed bolt to pass through.

Wedge   The wedge, or quoin (3), can also be made from a carriage side off-cut. File to 20 mm x 10 mm x 6 mm and drill a 2 mm hole in one end to receive the small handle which has been taper turned from 3 mm rod as shown. Complete by filing to a wedge shape.

Wheels   Mount a convenient length of 25 mm diameter rod (8) in the three-jaw chuck with approximately 30 mm protruding. Face off the end and centre drill out the 5 mm axle hole to a depth of 30 mm (i.e. sufficient for two wheels). Reduce the outside diameter to 24 mm for a length of 28 mm and further reduce to 9 mm in diameter for a length of 5 mm to make the inner hub of the first wheel. The inner face of the wheel is now bored out to a depth of 2 mm between the hub and rim, as shown on the drawing. Part off the wheel leaving a rim width of 7 mm.

Repeat these stages with the second wheel and then remount each wheel in turn, gripping the inner hub in the chuck (preferably using a four-jaw for extra security), and carefully bore out to a depth of 2 mm between outer hub and rim for the outer face. Finally, using a template, mark out, centre punch and drill eight 3 mm diameter holes in each wheel.

Assembly   Lacquer the exposed faces of each part, after polishing them with emery cloth. (Alternatively, if a brass barrel has been made, buff this to a high shine and lacquer. To finish the carriage in contrasting black, heat the steel parts almost to red heat and quench off in sump oil.) Coat the tie rod and bed bolt ends sparingly with epoxy resin and assemble the carriage sides with the bed and axletree in position. The wheels are held in position by two small rivets with a diameter of 1.6 mm, or escution pins which have been cut to a suitable length. Alternatively, if pin holes have not been drilled, the axletree ends may simply be flared over with a hammer.

Coat the central part of the trunnion sparingly with epoxy resin (and the dolphin ends, if made) and position in the barrel. The barrel itself is attached to the carriage by two split pins, opened sufficiently to pass over the trunnion and with their ends bent under the tie rod.

8-inch brass mortar, circa 1750

It has been shown that early gun design tended to fall into two distinct categories. One attempted to fire the largest and heaviest projectile and had a barrel which, because of its calibre, was limited in length. The other sought the greatest muzzle velocity and accuracy, and correspondingly required a long barrel of limited calibre in order to ensure sufficient strength. Quite fantastic sizes had been reached by the large calibre weapons which were called 'bombards' (hence the terms 'bombardier' and 'bombardment') and which, despite being crude and dangerous, led to the development of mortars in about 1400 for use in siege warfare. The term mortar itself may have derived from the chemist's mortar or the name of certain guns known at *meurtriers* or murderers. It was Charles VIII of France, who invaded Italy in 1495 with a large and well-organised siege train, who designated them separate weapons from cannon.

During a siege, apart from starving the poor occupants into surrender (which could take months or even years!), the only way to capture a well-designed fortress was to breach the walls with cannon fire and pour in large numbers of infantry. To breach walls – often up to 20 feet thick – was no easy task for the gunners, who had first to break the facing stones using solid shot and then, if necessary, disperse the debris with explosive shells. All this required pin-point accuracy from the longer guns, which could only be achieved by closing to within two or three hundred yards. Hence the value of supporting mortars, which could lob projectiles over the walls, causing panic and allowing other guns to continue their relentless pounding unhindered. Thus the Chief Firemaster, who had responsibility for the mortars and projectiles used in sieges, became a very important individual.

Before Lieutenant Shrapnel's invention of his famous shell, and its use in the Napoleonic Wars, solid shot remained the most popular for cannon. However, a variety of frightening projectiles

Early mortars at a siege

including exploding bombs, bags of stone, red-hot shot and fireballs were sent on high trajectories over defences by the mortars. The optimum elevation for this 'curved fire' was found to be 45° and so mortars were fixed at this angle from quite early times, their range being adjusted solely by varying the powder charge. Thus, although cartridges were widely used in most guns by 1800, loose powder had still to be retained for the mortars to adjust their range, which remained notoriously inaccurate. If an exploding bomb was chosen, its fuse required lighting separately before the charge – a somewhat hazardous undertaking until the obvious solution of allowing the powder flash to light it was discovered!

Like cannon, mortar barrels were made from wrought iron, bronze and cast iron in a variety of styles. An unusual forerunner found in the moat of Bodiam Castle, Sussex, is a combination of both wrought and cast iron. Some were even carved from stone, one was bored into the solid rock on Gibraltar, and the Russians are said to have carved them from ice! Apart from their short, stubby length (between one and four calibres) the principal feature of barrel design was the breech-end trunnion, so placed not to vary the elevation, but to distribute the immense downward thrust. Internally the bore reduced drastically at the powder chamber, and the shell rested on the resultant shoulder to avoid compressing the charge. At its simplest, the bed was no more than a few baulks of timber, hollowed for the breech and with a wedge in front for the fixed elevation.

Our 8-inch 'brass' mortar lies mid-way in the British inventory between the 4.4-inch (known as the 'four and two-fifths inch' or Cohorn Mortar) and the 13-inch described later. To Napoleon it was the ideal siege mortar, combining as it did fire power with manoeuvrability, but he should not be seen as having an exclusive claim to this: along with other innovations, Frederick the Great had, in the eighteenth century, already established the principal of using mortars in the field.

CONSTRUCTION (SCALE 1:15)

Because the original bed of the mortar was made of timber, the model bed may be made from a suitably close-grained hardwood, such as mahogany, as shown in the photograph. Alternatively, the model engineer might wish to work exclusively in steel, and this is referred to in the cutting lists. Less experienced metalworkers could omit the capsquares and fittings or, as a compromise, make only simplified capsquares, held in place by adhesive or rivets.

Barrel Saw off a 52 mm length of 25 mm rod (1) and face off either end in the lathe to a finished length of 50 mm. Mark out and centre punch 7 mm from the breech end and, holding the work in a machine vice, drill out an 8 mm diameter trunnion hole.

Remount the piece well into the three-jaw chuck, centre drill the muzzle end and drill out the bore to 12 mm in diameter and 20 mm in depth. Reposition so that approximately 10 mm of the breech end may be gripped in the chuck, and support the bore on a revolving centre in the tailstock. Now parallel turn the barrel to a diameter of 24 mm almost up to the chuck. Further reduce the muzzle end to 20 mm in diameter, then set the top-slide to 10° and taper turn the chase between the muzzle swell and the central reinforce, as shown.

Reverse the work in the chuck and, with approximately 12 mm of the breech protruding, reduce it to 22 mm in diameter up to the central reinforce. Finally, progressively round the breech to a radius of 11 mm, taking particular care around the trunnion hole. The trunnion itself (2) is made from 8 mm diameter rod faced off to a length of 45 mm.

Bed Saw off three 92 mm lengths of 16 mm square bar and file the ends square to a length of 90 mm. Hold the three side by side in the vice and mark out a curve across the rear end of the bed. Hacksaw the waste off the outer two bars and file them to shape individually, then grip all three together in the vice to finish to a smooth curve.

Now hold the outer two (6) together, with their top surfaces face to face in the machine vice, and centre punch and drill out a trunnion hole 8 mm in diameter, thereby forming a semi-circle in each. Next, mark out four 3 mm capstan holes on the outer face of

8" BRASS MORTAR

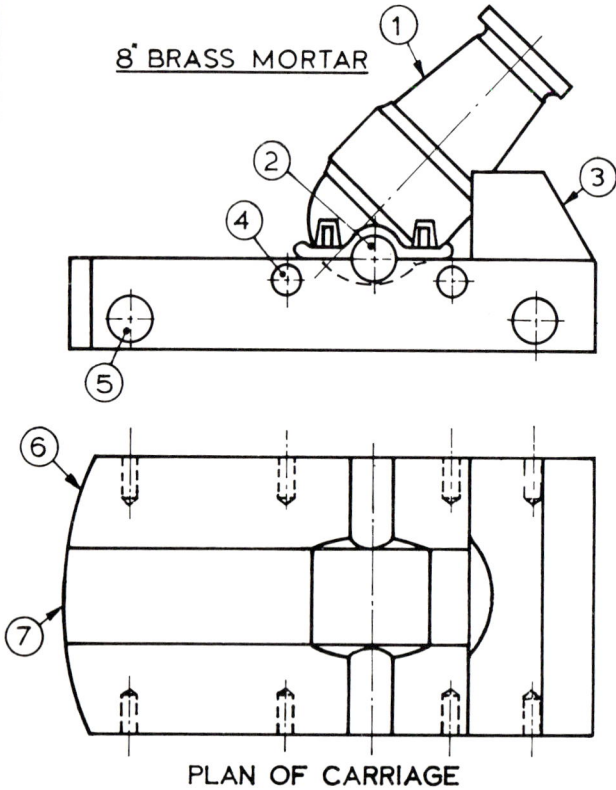

PLAN OF CARRIAGE

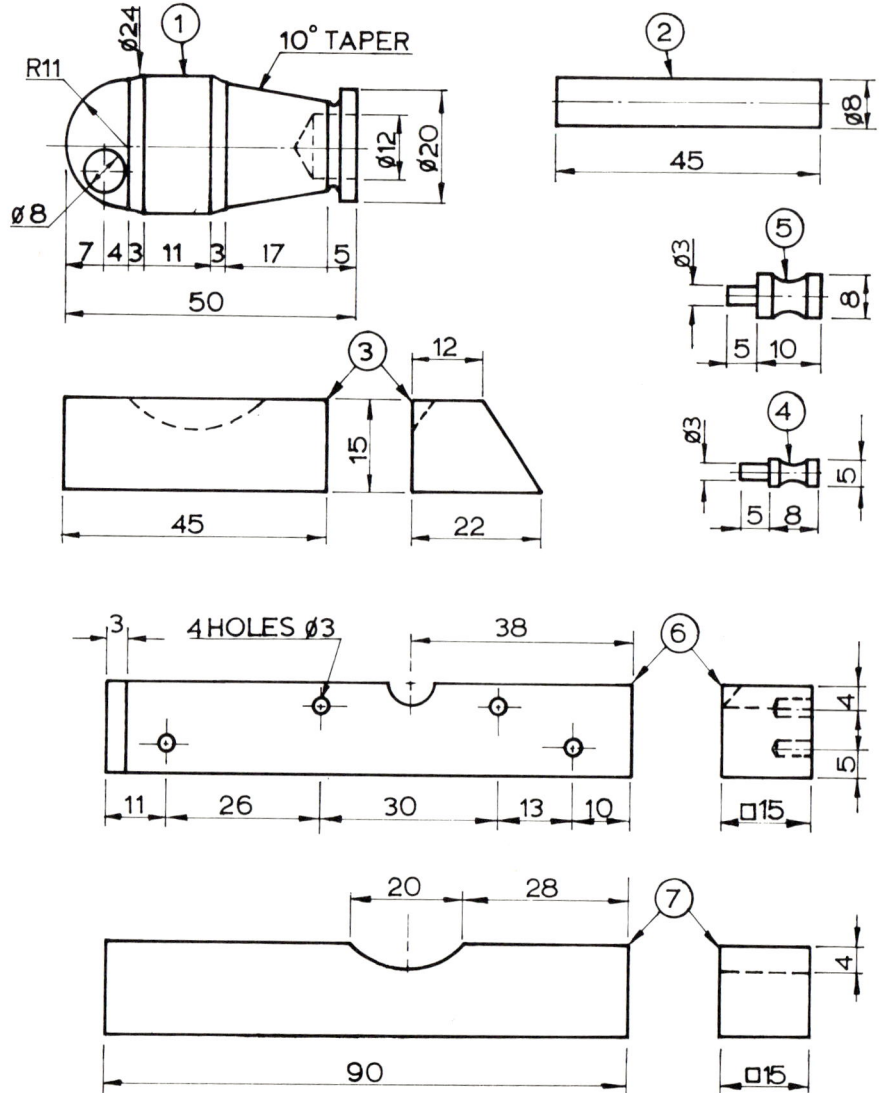

R11
Ø24
10° TAPER
Ø8
Ø12
Ø20
7 | 4 | 3 | 11 | 3 | 17 | 5
50

45
Ø8

Ø3
5 | 10
8

Ø3
5 | 8
5

3
15
12
45
22

4 HOLES Ø3
38
11 | 26 | 30 | 13 | 10
4
5
□15

20 | 28
90
4
□15

SCALE 4:5

ITEM	NAME	NO.	CUTTING SIZE
1	BARREL	1	25 DIA. ROD
2	TRUNNION	1	46 x 8 DIA. ROD
3	REST	1	46 x 22 x 15
4	CAPSTAN	4	6 DIA. ROD
5	CAPSTAN	4	10 DIA. ROD
6	BED (L+R)	2	92 x 16 SQUARE
7	BED	1	92 x 16 SQUARE

each piece and drill to a depth of approximately 7 mm. Finally, file off the inner corners around the trunnion hollows to receive the large rounded breech of the mortar. The middle section (7) of the bed is hollowed with a half-round file to a depth of 4 mm to accommodate the rounded breech.

The rest or transom (3) is made from a 46 mm length of 22 mm x 15 mm bar filed to a length of 45 mm. The angled front can be formed by hacksawing and filing, or by the shaper or milling machine. A hollow filed in the top rear edge is also required to support the barrel at 45° as shown.

Capstans   The four large capstans (5) are turned from 10 mm diameter rod. Mount the first piece in the lathe with approximately 20 mm protruding and face off the end. Parallel turn to a diameter of 8 mm, and further reduce to a 3 mm diameter for a length of 5 mm. Now cut the groove with a round-nose tool and part off the piece to an overall length of 15 mm. Alternatively, hacksaw it off, and remount it in the lathe to face off the cut surface. Repeat the operations for the remaining three capstans.

The four small capstans (4) are similarly turned from 6 mm diameter rod to the dimensions shown. Because of the small diameters involved, light cuts should be taken.

Capsquares   Saw two lengths of square bar 28 mm x 6 mm x 6 mm and file to a length of 27 mm. Mount side by side in the machine vice, centre punch on their joint centre line and carefully drill the 8 mm trunnion hole to form a semi-circle in each. Using a sheet metal template, mark out the top curve on each capsquare and file to shape. Finally, mark out the pintle slots with their centres 16 mm apart, drill out the waste with a 2 mm diameter drill and finish with a square needle file.

If simplified capsquares and fittings are to be made, omit the square pintle holes and drill two 3 mm diameter holes in each capsquare to take 3 mm snap head rivets, the heads of which have been filed to look like pintles.

Pintles and pins   The pintles are cut from 2 mm steel sheet. After they have been filed to shape, drill a 1.2 mm hole in each and file square to accept the tapered pin. Now round off the lower half of each pintle to 2 mm in diameter for a length of 6 mm to fit a 2 mm hole drilled in the bed. The pins are cut from 1.2 mm steel sheet and filed to a slight taper.

Assembly   Polish all the external faces of the metal parts with emery cloth and coat the sides of the three bed pieces sparingly with epoxy resin. Align these carefully, and squeeze them together in the vice, wiping away any surplus adhesive which may ooze from the joints. When the adhesive is set, similarly fix the transom and then the capstans in position. If the bed is made from hardwood, use an appropriate wood adhesive to join the parts, and lightly glasspaper and polish. Now coat the trunnion sparingly with epoxy resin and slide it into the barrel. When the resin is set, assemble the barrel on the bed and lock the trunnion down with the capsquares. If pintles have been made, fit these into 2 mm diameter holes drilled 16 mm apart in the bed; if rivets are used then 3 mm diameter holes are required.

Naval long 12-pounder, circa 1750

For several centuries after the dawn of artillery its exploitation at sea proceeded relatively slowly. Traditional naval tactics involved grappling alongside the enemy before hand-to-hand fighting could ensure his defeat. In fact, as late as the nineteenth century the Royal Navy preferred long-range broadsides to be followed by close-quarter combat. Originally, cannon were placed in high castles (hence the term forecastle or fo'c'sle) built for archers to shoot down from, but eventually they were positioned nearer the vessel's water-line for improved stability and seaworthiness.

Prior to the development of specialist warships with lines of gunports, in the sixteenth century, the evolution of naval cannon lagged behind that of land artillery: there was quite an assortment available, but it was not expected to be used as intensely or as frequently as that on land. If a ship did sink it would be lost entirely. However, it was soon standardised and refined to efficiency for the new Navy and attention shifted from the barrel to the carriage.

Originally, the barrel had simply slid back along a grooved block. It was realised that increased mass would reduce the violent recoil, so a form of trough was designed for both barrel and block to recoil together. This in turn led to the truck carriage to which wheels ('trucks') had been added to facilitate handling and loading and to reduce friction with the deck. Elm was the timber used, as it both absorbed shock and resisted splintering. The wheels were banded with iron although this could in itself be dangerous if the cannon was struck and so was subsequently abandoned. Unfortunately, although the wooden truck design remained in service until the advent of breech loading weapons, it was hardly the ideal solution; the breeching rope was primitive and the assembly jumped violently on firing – and if the lashings gave way, as they might well do in a storm, the gun itself could become a three-ton projectile!

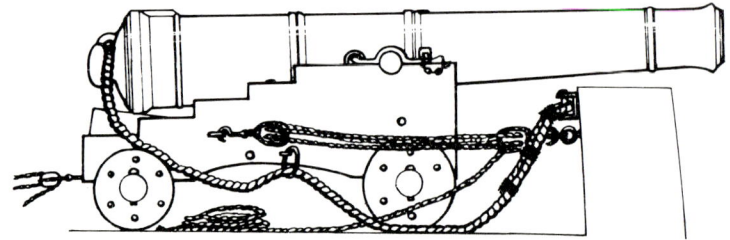

Long 12-pounder, showing breeching rope and side tackle

At sea, cast iron became the principal material used for guns, apart from the heavy brass mortars. Improved foundry practice ensured that the Royal Navy's cannon were somewhat more reliable than their French counterparts, which were still regarded with apprehension by the sailors. One revolutionary development in barrel manufacture had still to come: the invention in 1739 of the cannon boring machine, by the Swiss gun-founder Maritz of Geneva. Henceforth, instead of being cast hollow around a core, iron guns could be bored from the solid, giving greater strength and accuracy (and for a cost one-eighth that of bronze). Thus, during the eighteenth century a more or less universal method of design, manufacture and nomenclature was established. As shown on page 38 the barrel, after narrowing behind the muzzle swell, gradually flared outwards to the breech, providing progressively more metal towards the place of explosion. Essentially, there were three principal sections: chase, second reinforce and first reinforce ('reinforce' signifying thicker metal).

The example shown is the characteristic long 12-pounder dating from the late eighteenth century, which has the classic features and proportions so beloved of model-makers. Variations on this design must have graced many a fine desk over the years.

Remember that almost 200 years before, the English Navy's preference for such long guns had enabled it to defeat the Spanish Armada while remaining out of range itself. However, during the nineteenth century, the relatively small bores of such weapons could no longer sink the thickly-clad men-of-war until the advent of our later example, the aptly named 'Smasher'.

CONSTRUCTION (SCALE 1:15)

The ship's cannon has always been a firm favourite with model engineers. Usually a shorter version is chosen for construction, but the long 12-pounder with its elegant proportions makes a fitting addition to our collection. The model in the photograph is made entirely of mild steel, although the reader might wish to substitute mahogany or oak for the carriage, and finish the barrel and fittings in a contrasting black to represent the original iron-work. As with the previous model, less experienced metalworkers could omit the capsquares and minor fittings or, as a compromise, make only a simplified capsquare held in place by rivets.

Barrel Saw off a 200 mm length of 25 mm diameter rod (1) and mount well into the three-jaw chuck. Face off the end, centre drill and drill out the bore to a diameter of 8 mm and a depth of approximately 10 mm.

Remove the piece from the lathe, centre punch 105 mm from the muzzle end for the trunnion hole and, holding it in a machine vice, drill an 8 mm diameter hole to a depth of 5 or 6 mm. Now reposition the work so that the hole is off centre and drill right through.

Remount in the chuck, gripping approximately 25 mm and supporting the muzzle end on a revolving centre. Parallel turn the exposed length to 24 mm in diameter, then further reduce this to 21 mm between the base ring, the vent field astragal and the first reinforce ring. Now set the top-slide to an angle of 3° and taper turn between the muzzle swell, muzzle astragal and the second and first reinforce rings. Turn each band to its largest diameter, first using a round-nosed tool and then finishing the corners with a knife tool. The muzzle swell is formed by carefully manipulating the top-slide and cross-slide simultaneously.

Reverse the piece in the chuck, protecting the base ring, the astragal and the first reinforce with a band of copper. Face off and turn down to 8 mm in diameter for the button, then carefully form the breech ogee, the neck fillet and, last of all, the button.

The trunnion (2) is made from 8 mm diameter rod faced off to a length of 38 mm.

Carriage sides Use a card or sheet metal template to mark out the sides on two 102 mm x 32 mm x 6 mm strips (3). After filing them to length, clamp the two side by side in a machine vice and ensure that they are supported underneath. Centre punch the trunnion hole and drill out to 8 mm in diameter, forming a semi-circle in each side. Now drill out two 3 mm bolt holes in one side and use this as a guide to drill out the second side.

Shape the outer contours of the sides, removing the waste metal by hacksawing, drilling and filing as appropriate. If a vertical milling machine is available, the steps can be machined in both sides at once. However, the axle slots must be machined separately, requiring the machine vice to be set at an angle of 2° to accommodate the taper in the assembled carriage. A slight easing of the trunnion hollows and bolt holes with round files should also be carried out because of this taper. Finally, drill 1.2 mm holes for the pintles and 2 mm holes for the U-bolts, if these are to be fitted.

Axles and rest Both axles (7 and 8) are turned from 80 mm

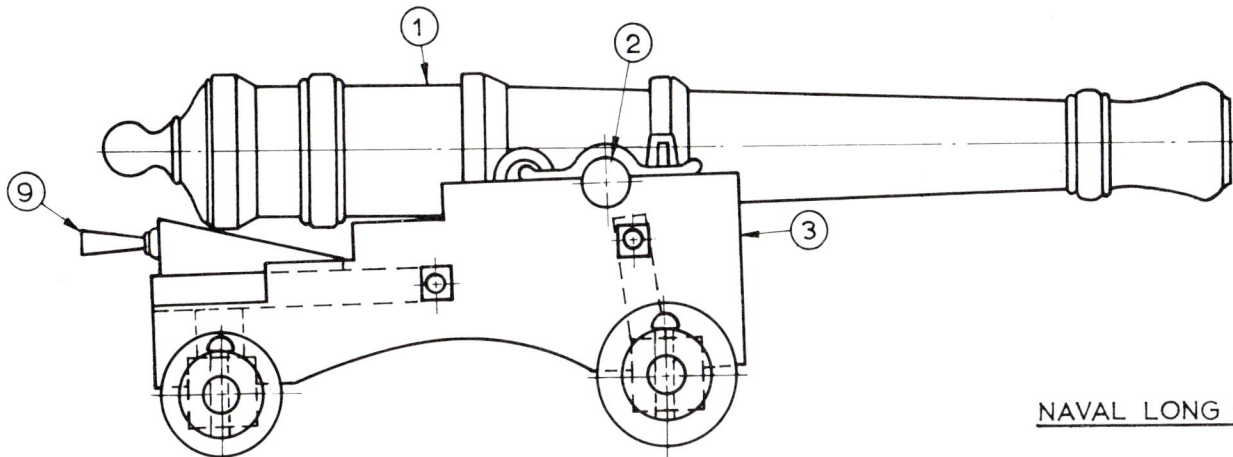

NAVAL LONG 12-POUNDER

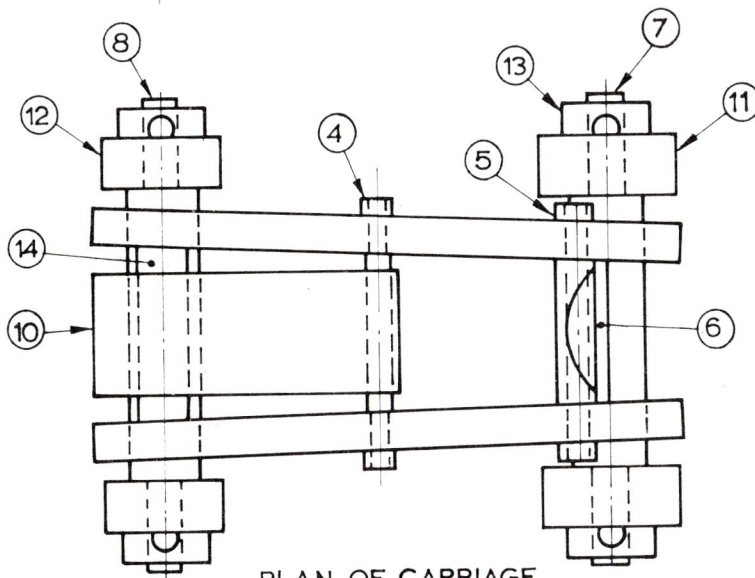

PLAN OF CARRIAGE

SCALE 4:5

ITEM	NAME	NO.	CUTTING SIZE
1	BARREL	1	25 DIA. ROD
2	TRUNNION	1	40 x 8 DIA. ROD
3	SIDE	2	102 x 32 x 6 STRIP
4	BED BOLT	1	47 x 4 DIA. ROD
5	TRANSOM B'T	1	45 x 3 DIA. ROD
6	TRANSOM	1	25 x 20 x 6 STRIP
7	FRONT AXLE	1	80 x 12 SQUARE
8	REAR AXLE	1	80 x 12 SQUARE
9	WEDGE	1	31 x 10 SQUARE
10	BED	1	54 x 20 x 6 STRIP
11	WHEEL	2	25 DIA. ROD
12	WHEEL	2	25 DIA. ROD
13	WASHER	4	16 DIA. ROD
14	REST	1	32 x 8 SQUARE

THE PARTS OF A CANNON BARREL C.1780

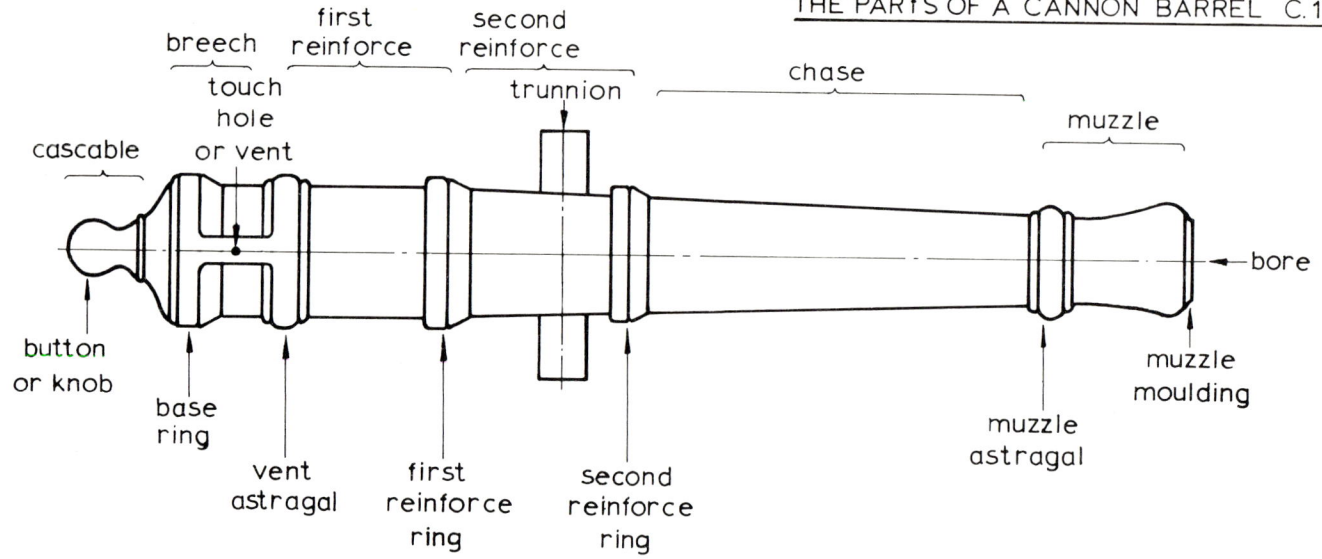

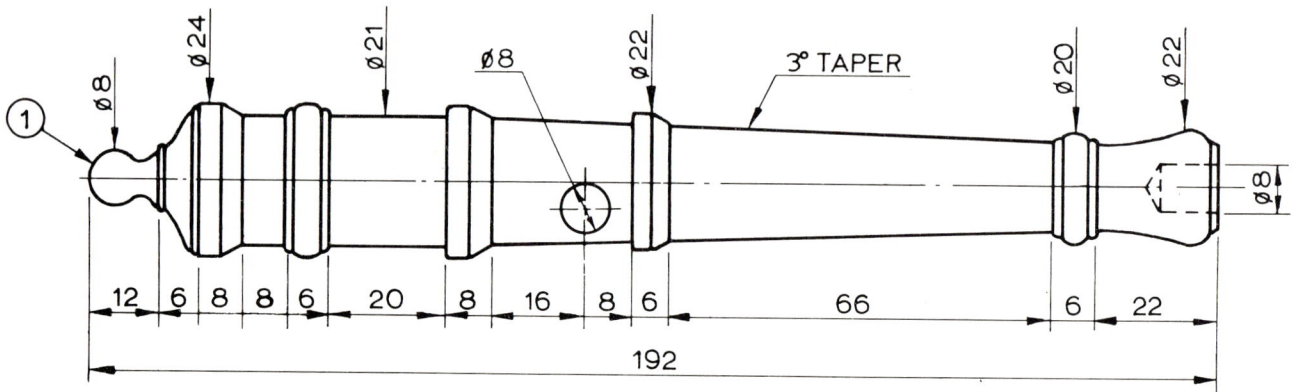

cascable

breech

first reinforce

second reinforce

chase

muzzle

touch hole or vent

trunnion

bore

button or knob

base ring

vent astragal

first reinforce ring

second reinforce ring

muzzle astragal

muzzle moulding

① Ø8 Ø24 Ø21 Ø8 Ø22 3° TAPER Ø20 Ø22 Ø8

② Ø8

38

12 6 8 8 6 20 8 16 8 6 66 6 22

192

NAVAL LONG 12-POUNDER BARREL

PLAN VIEW

SCALE 4:5

lengths of 12 mm square bar. Mount both pieces in the four-jaw chuck, face off the ends to a length of 78 mm and reduce the front axle to a 6 mm diameter for a length of 16 mm at either end. Similarly reduce the rear axle to 6 mm in diameter, but for the shorter length of 14 mm.

Centre punch, mount in a machine vice and drill holes for the wheel pins 3 mm in diameter and 12 mm from the shoulder in the front axle and 10 mm in the rear one. (These are not required if the wheels are to be held in place by riveting over the axle ends.)

The bed rest (14), which lies along the rear axletree, is cut to a length of 29 mm from 8 mm square bar and then filed to an angle of 2° to fit the taper of the carriage sides when the cannon is assembled.

Bed The bed or platform (10) is shaped from a strip 54 mm x 20 mm x 6 mm. File both ends square to an overall length of 52 mm, mark out the centre of the bolt hole 3 mm from one end and drill out to a diameter of 4 mm.

Transom Saw off a 27 mm length of 20 mm x 6 mm strip (6) and file both ends square to a length of 25 mm. Mark out the bolt hole centre 3 mm from the top edge and drill through a 3 mm diameter hole. Now angle the ends to 2° to fit the taper of the carriage sides. In addition, angle the bottom edge to 7° to lie flush with the front axletree and file a hollow in the top edge to accommodate the barrel when it is depressed for low angle shots.

Bed bolt Saw off a 47 mm length of 4 mm diameter rod (4) and face off both ends, in the lathe, to a final length of 45 mm. Now reduce the diameter at either end slightly to 3 mm for a length of 9 mm and thread this M3. The two nuts can be cut from off-cuts filed to 5 mm square by 3 mm thick, which are then drilled and tapped M3 while they are held in the four-jaw chuck.

Transom bolt This can be made from 3 mm diameter wire (5) or welding rod, cut and filed to a length of 45 mm, and similarly threaded M3 at either end to take square nuts made in the manner described above.

Wedge The wedge or quoin (9) is shaped from 10 mm square bar. Cut and file the ends square to a length of 30 mm and then mark out and drill a 2 mm diameter hole in one of the ends to receive the handle. The latter is turned to shape from 4 mm diameter rod. Finally, mark out, hacksaw and file the wedge to shape.

Wheels, washers and pins All four wheels are turned from 25 mm diameter rod: the front pair (11) to 10 mm thick and the rear ones (12) to 8 mm thick. Mount a convenient length of rod in the three-jaw chuck with 35 mm protruding. Face off, centre drill and drill out the axle hole to 6 mm in diameter and 25 mm deep. Now parallel turn the wheel to a diameter of 24 mm for a length of 30 mm and carefully part off the two larger wheels. Reposition the rod in the chuck and repeat the process for the two smaller ones.

The washers (13) are turned in a similar manner from 16 mm diameter rod but, being narrower, all four can be parted off without having to reposition the rod in the chuck. Mount a convenient length in the chuck with approximately 35 mm protruding, face off, centre drill and drill out an axle hole 6 mm in diameter to a depth of 35 mm. Parallel turn to an outer diameter of 15 mm and part off to a thickness of 5 mm each. Complete by securing each washer firmly in the machine vice and drilling a 3 mm hole across its diameter to take the wheel pin.

The four wheel pins are made from 3 mm diameter snap head rivets, polished with emery cloth until they are a push fit through the washers and axles.

Capsquares Saw off two lengths of square bar 3 mm x 6 mm x 6 mm and file to a length of 30 mm. Mount them side by side in the machine vice, centre punch on their joint centre-line 17 mm from the front end and carefully drill an 8 mm

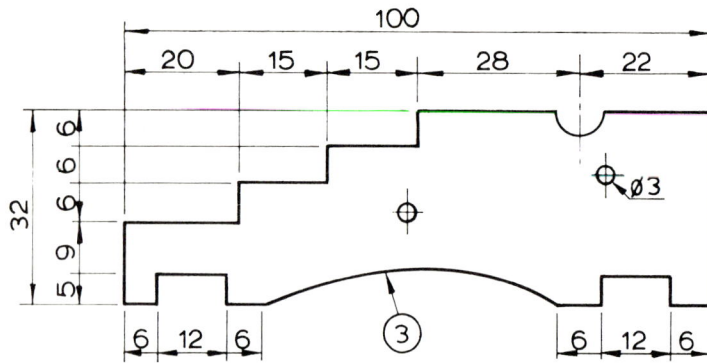

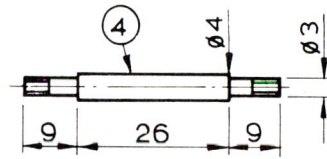

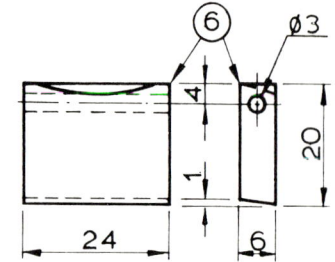

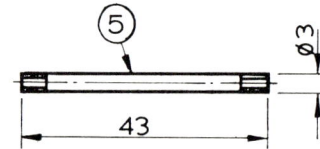

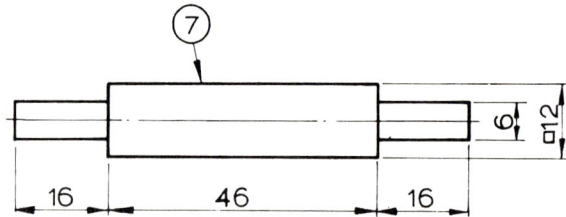

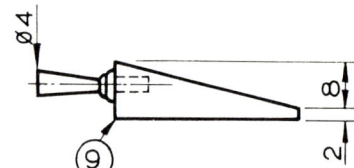

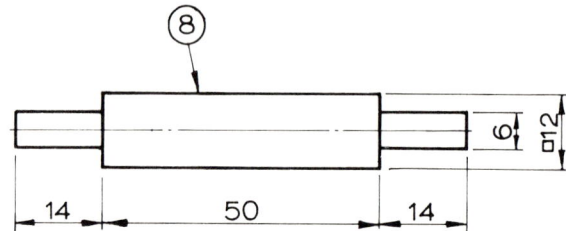

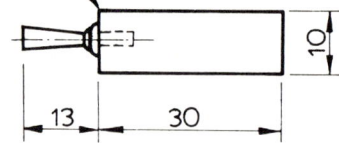

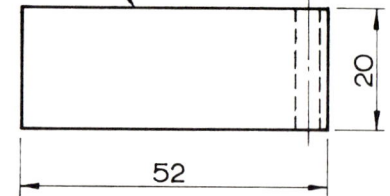

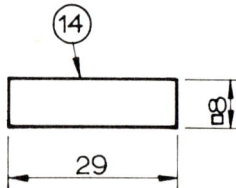

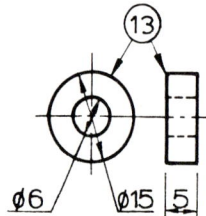

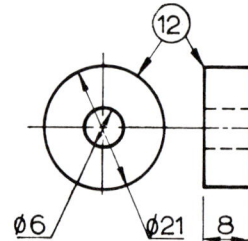

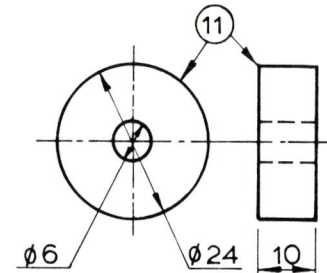

100

20 15 15 28 22

32 6 6 6 6 9 5

6 12 6 ③ 6 12 6

Ø3

④ Ø4 Ø3

9 26 9

⑤ Ø3

43

⑥ Ø3

4 1 20

24 6

⑦ 6 □12

16 46 16

⑧ 6 □12

14 50 14

Ø4 ⑨ 8 2 10

13 30

⑩ Ø4 6 3 20

52

⑭ □8

29

⑬ Ø6 Ø15 5

⑫ Ø6 Ø21 8

⑪ Ø6 Ø24 10

SCALE 4:5

40

trunnion hole to form a semi-circle in each. Using a sheet metal template, mark out the top curve on each capsquare and file to shape. Now mark out the pintle and U-bolt holes 10 mm either side of the trunnion hole centre. Drill out the holes to a diameter of 2 mm and file the forward ones square to slot over the pintles.

Pintles and pins   The pintles are cut from 2 mm steel sheet. After filing them to shape, drill a 1.2 mm hole in each and file square to take the tapered pin. Now round off the lower half of each pintle to a diameter of 2 mm for a length of 6 mm to fit the 2 mm hole drilled in the carriage. The pins are cut from 1.2 mm steel sheet and filed to a slight taper to wedge into the pintle holes.

U-Bolts   Three pairs of U-bolts can be fitted: one pair to hold down the rear ends of the capsquares and two pairs for the breeching tackle. Each U-bolt is bent to shape from a 20 mm length of 2 mm diameter wire. Bend round a 5 mm diameter rod to fit into pairs of 2 mm diameter holes, drilled with centres 6 mm apart to a depth of 5 mm.

Assembly   Polish each part with emery cloth and coat all exposed surfaces with lacquer. If hardwood has been used for the carriage, finish this part with fine glasspaper and polish with semi-matt polyurethane or wax. To give the barrel and fittings a black finish which will contrast with the wood, heat the steel almost to red heat and quench off in sump oil.

Slot the bolts in position through the carriage sides, transom and bed, and screw on the nuts. Then coat the appropriate faces sparingly with epoxy resin and fit the axles and bed rest in position. Also coat the U-bolts, pintles and trunnion and position them in their holes. Finally, assemble the barrel and wheels on the carriage and lock into place with the appropriate pins.

13-inch brass mortar, circa 1790

The 13-inch mortar was the largest calibre weapon ever in general use, although the largest one ever constructed was the 36-inch Mallet's mortar, which cost £14 000. Mortars were reserved essentially for siege battles on account of their weight and the length of time it took to set them up. Nevertheless, this was a common form of warfare until mid-Victorian times, when mortars were still widely used. (Indeed, the technicalities of siege warfare and fortifications had been a necessary study for kings and princes as well as generals, a study which often involved the use of scale models to provide realism.) At the siege of Sebastopol, in the Crimean War, British 13-inch mortars were continually in action, while in the Indian Mutiny of 1857, 8- and 10-inch mortars maintained a hail of fire during the breaching of the walls of Delhi. In fact, they became a popular weapon against the massive Indian mud forts, causing chaos in the crowded interiors. Their high trajectories even led to their exploitation in mountain warfare before howitzers were introduced.

The 13-inch mortar shares many features of barrel design with the 8-inch: a large rounded breech with integral trunnions, a wide central reinforce with dolphins, and a short chase between reinforce and muzzle swell. However, these owe their inheritance more to cannon design than to scientific research. As John Muller, Professor of Fortifications and Artillery at the Royal Military Academy, Woolwich, remarked in his *Treatise of Artillery*, 'A reinforce . . . only overloads the mortar with a heap of useless metal'.

The bed, however, is somewhat more elaborate than that of the 8-inch, having two stout wooden sides connected by bolts and a transom to support the reinforce. It would, in turn, be mounted on a substantial level platform for accurate traversing. The exploding shell weighed 200 lb and to facilitate loading a crane and winch could be fitted to one of its sides, although, as it was cast hollow for the explosive, two men could just about handle it. Maximum range was 1300 yards but this was increased to an incredible 4100 yards in another version, the 13-inch sea service mortar.

Large mortars had become such a necessary part of land artillery that inevitably they, too, were adopted by navies in the late seventeenth century, particularly since transport did not present so acute a problem. At sea they were able to play a vital role in laying siege to ports and coastal towns, supplementing the cannon fire of men-of-war. Abraham Duquesne, the French naval hero, first conceived the use of mortars at sea against the pirate town of Algiers in 1682; the English used them against the French when they attacked St. Malo in 1693. However, the immense downward recoil of the guns did demand a special kind of ship, strong enough to absorb shock yet shallow enough to sail close inland. As a result, vessels were specially constructed and strengthened for the purpose. They were about 70 feet long and became known as bomb ketches or bomb vessels, and, in this country, H.M. Bombs, these last being given such delightfully graphic names as *Thunder*, *Infernal* and *Blast*.

Normally each vessel would sport a 13-inch and 10-inch mortar mounted on solid wooden beds braced with heavy transoms, with the occasional 6-pounder for personal defence. The weight of the brass 13-inch was over four tons compared to the $1\frac{1}{4}$ tons of the land-based equivalent but, as noted above, there was an equivalent increase in range. Despite the large size of the purpose-built ships, space was restricted, with an ever-present risk of fire. Wooden screens had to be suspended over the vents to absorb flash, and wet tarpaulins draped over the magazine hatches, with substantial bulkheads separating the guns from the hatches. At first, no accommodation was provided for a crew who, it would appear, lived in an escorting vessel, only manning

H.M. Bomb when it was required for action. Eventually, in the early nineteenth century, larger vessels were suitably appointed and manned by the newly formed Royal Marine Artillery, and they remained in service until the late 1860s.

The effectiveness of 13-inch mortars against ships themselves was also realised and, well into the late nineteenth century, coastal defences included them on the assumption that the decks of heavily armoured warships were more vulnerable than their sides.

CONSTRUCTION (SCALE 1:20)

Although steel has been used throughout in the photographed model, apart from the barrel rest, the reader might wish to substitute brass for the barrel and a close-grained hardwood, such as mahogany, for the carriage sides. Less experienced metalworkers could omit the capsquares and minor fittings or, as a compromise, make only a simplified capsquare held in place by adhesive or rivets.

Barrel Saw off a 62 mm length of 25 mm diameter rod (1) and mount well into the three-jaw chuck. Face off the end, centre drill, pilot drill and drill out the bore of the barrel to a diameter of 16 mm and a depth of 20 mm. Reverse in the chuck and face off the breech end to give an overall length of 60 mm. Using the lathe tool, scribe a centre line down each side of the barrel and centre punch 10 mm from the breech end. Now, holding the work in the machine vice, drill out a 8 mm hole for the trunnion.

Return the piece to the chuck, leaving approximately 40 mm protruding and the muzzle end supported on a revolving centre. Parallel turn to a diameter of 24 mm for approximately 38 mm and reduce the chase between the muzzle and the central reinforce to a diameter of 20 mm. Now carefully finish the rings of the muzzle and reinforce as shown in the drawing. Reverse the work in the chuck leaving 30 mm protruding, reduce the breech to a diameter of 20 mm up to the central reinforce and carefully turn the rings on this side of the reinforce. Finally, round the breech end to a 10 mm radius, taking care when turning around the trunnion hole.

The trunnion (2) is made from 8 mm diameter rod, faced off to a length of 38 mm. If dolphins are to be added to the barrel they can be bent to their U-shapes from 28 mm lengths of 2 mm diameter wire to fit into four holes drilled 6 mm apart in the central reinforce, as shown in the photograph.

Carriage sides Mark out the two sides (6) on 87 mm x 25 mm x 6 mm strips, using a card or sheet metal template. Centre punch and drill out four 3 mm rod holes in one of the sides, and also a 6 mm diameter hole in the transom groove to facilitate shaping it out. Use this first side as a guide to drilling out the second one.

Hacksaw off the waste metal and file each side to shape, using a square or hand file for the corners and a round file for the trunnion hollows. Finally, clamp both sides together in the vice to complete the shaping. When drilling and filing, short pins of 3 mm rod should be placed in the holes to position the two sides accurately.

Tie Rods The four tie rods (4) are turned from 6 mm diameter rod. Two should be faced off to an overall length of 38 mm and then reduced to 3 mm in diameter at either end for a distance of 6 mm. The two shorter ones, which the capstans butt against, are faced off to a length of 32 mm and reduced to a diameter of 3 mm for a distance of 3 mm at either end.

Capstans Mount a length of 6 mm diameter rod (5) in the lathe with approximately 20 mm protruding. Face off the end and reduce to 3 mm in diameter for a distance of 3 mm. Now cut the

13" BRASS MORTAR

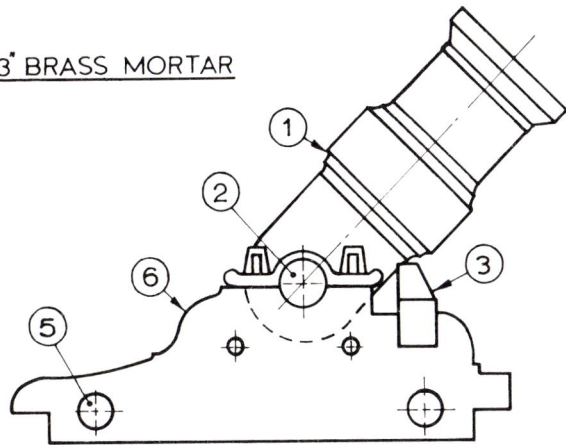

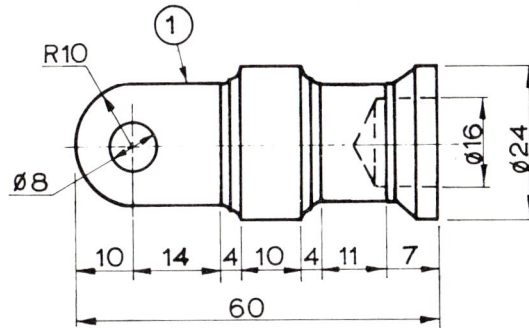

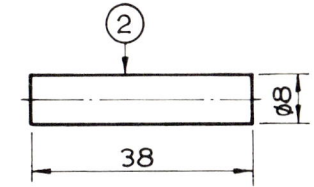

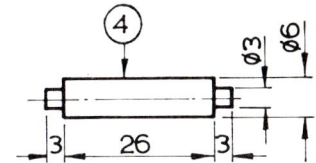

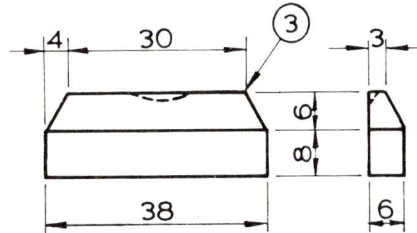

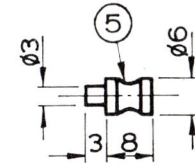

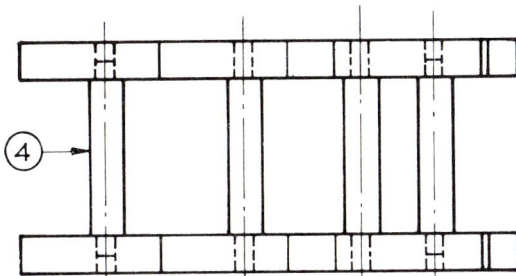

PLAN OF CARRIAGE

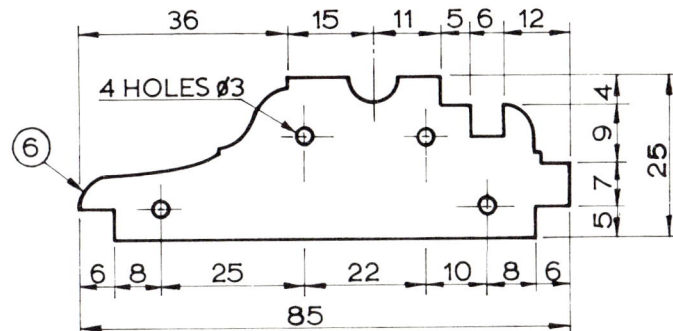

ITEM	NAME	NO.	CUTTING SIZE
1	BARREL	1	25 DIA. ROD
2	TRUNNION	1	40 x 8 DIA. ROD
3	BARREL REST	1	40 x 15 x 6
4	TIE ROD	4	40 x 6 DIA. ROD
5	CAPSTAN	4	6 DIA. ROD
6	SIDE	2	87 x 25 x 6

4 HOLES Ø3

SCALE 4:5

groove and part of the first capstan to an overall length of 11 mm. Alternatively, hacksaw it off and remount in the lathe to face off the cut surface. Repeat the operations for the remaining three capstans.

Barrel rest   The barrel rest or transom (3) is filed to shape from a piece of 40 mm x 15 mm x 6 mm steel or close-grained hardwood. File the ends square to an overall length of 38 mm. Mark out the bevels using spring dividers, and file to shape. Complete the piece by filing the hollow for the barrel to rest in.

Capsquares   Saw two lengths of square bar 28 mm x 6 mm x 6 mm and file to a length of 27 mm. Mount them side by side in the machine vice, centre punch on their joint centre line and carefully drill the 8 mm trunnion hole to form a semi-circle in each. Using a sheet metal template, mark out the top curve to each capsquare and file to shape. Finally, mark out the pintle slots with their centres 16 mm apart, drill out the waste with a 2 mm diameter drill and finish with a square needle file.

If simplified capsquares and fittings are to be made, omit the square pintle holes and drill two 3 mm diameter holes in each capsquare and carriage side to accept 3 mm snap head rivets, the heads of which have been filed with flats to look like pintles.

Pintles and pins   The pintles are cut from 2 mm steel sheet. After filing to shape drill a 1.2 mm hole in each and file square to take the tapered pin. Now round off the lower half of each pintle to a diameter of 2 mm for a length of 6 mm to fit into a 2 mm hole drilled in the carriage side.

The pins are cut from 1.2 mm steel sheet and filed to a slight taper to wedge into the pintle holes.

Assembly   Polish each metal part with emery cloth and lacquer the exposed surfaces. Coat the rod ends and capstans sparingly with epoxy resin and assemble the carriage. Next coat the middle of the trunnion and the dolphin ends with epoxy resin and press them into position in the barrel. Finally, position the transom and lock the barrel trunnions onto the carriage with the capsquares, pintles and pins. Scale model engineers may wish to embellish the mortar by the addition of jewellery chain to the pins, 6 mm diameter ring bolts to the transom, and eye bolts to the carriage as shown in the photograph on page 43.

32-pounder carronade, circa 1790

Fondly known as 'The Smasher', the carronade was a specialised form of gun which originated from the Carron Foundry at Falkirk, Scotland, in the 1770s. It was designed by the works manager, Mr. Gascoigne, and Lieutenant-General Robert Melville. Initially called a 'Gasconade', it embodied the first major change to barrel design since the 16th century, and, after various trials, was accepted into the British artillery in 1779, remaining in service until the middle of the nineteenth century. Interestingly, Samuel Pepys' diary of a century before the invention mentions an experimental gun, the 'Punchinello', similar in concept but never adopted, probably because of unreliable manufacturing technology. A later treatise by the brilliant Benjamin Robins argued the theory of such a gun, but it took Carrons to actually make it. Eventually the Americans were to develop the 'Columbian' which improved on the carronade by combining many of the advantages of traditional cannon with those of the new weapon.

Since they were designed to operate in confined spaces – for example, in garrisons and ships – carronades had short, thin-walled barrels with relatively small chambers for gunpowder, like mortars, which limited the amount of charge powder and also the range. But this was more than compensated for by their lightness, ease of handling and, most importantly, their ability to fire disproportionately large-calibre shells. Because the shells were hollow they disintegrated on impact, so that even small carronades were extremely dangerous to enemy personnel. At short range the big 68-pounders were capable of tearing massive irregular openings, rather than small holes, in what had otherwise been almost impregnable ships' sides. This, coupled with their rapid rate of fire manned by only two or three men, meant that their involvement could be decisive, particularly in close-quarter actions. This particularly suited the British Navy, the only problem being that a captain's pay was based on the number

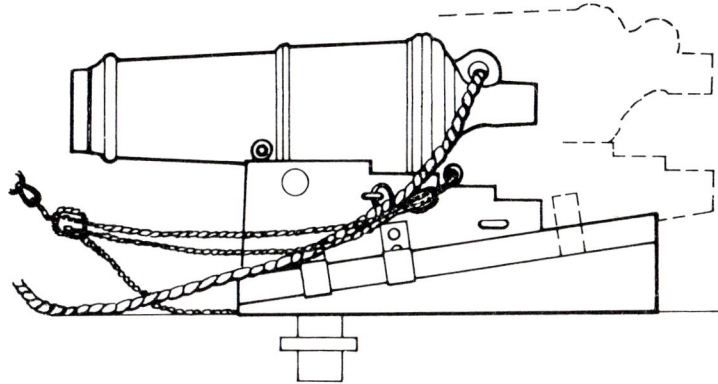

Carronade mounted on inclined carriage slide

of guns a ship carried – and carronades were not to be included in the calculation!

Whatever their size, from 68- down to 6-pounders, all carronades had uniform features and proportions, their fire power resulting principally from reduced windage (i.e. the energy lost through the space between shot and barrel walls), which was excessive in most other British guns. At Carron's the use of John 'Cast Iron' Wilkinson's new boring machines made it possible to work to much finer tolerances than had previously been possible. (Such machines were to contribute further to engineering progress by accurately boring out the cylinders of James Watt's famous steam engines.) Thus our 32-pounder carronade had a barrel just over 4 feet long, weighed under 7 cwt and, of course, fired a shot weighing 32 lb. In comparison, a conventional 4-foot cannon could only manage a 3 lb shot and a 17-cwt cannon a 6 to 9 lb shot.

Although mainly associated with the Navy, large numbers of carronades were used in forts and coastal defences, and the 32-

pounder in the photograph is shown mounted on a small iron garrison carriage. One of its important features was the lack of trunnions on the thin-walled barrel. Instead, a single cast lug was incorporated which would fit a slide carriage at sea or such a carriage on land. Invariably, the gun was unsteady when fired, further necessitating that the charge be kept low. To ease loading in restricted surroundings the muzzle was cast with a funnel opening, which also helped disperse the flames following a shot and so reduced the ever-present danger of fire in confined spaces.

Despite these limitations, so pleased were Carron's with the overwhelming success of their new gun that they presented General Melville with a model inscribed 'Gift of the Carron Company to Lieutenant-General Melville, inventor of the Smashers and lesser carronades for solid, ship, shell, and carcass shot, etc: First used against French ships in 1779'. Gascoigne, in turn, reaped his own reward, for in 1779 he emigrated to Russia and installed the great cannon factory at Petrozarodsky near Lake Onega, gaining high honours and salary from Catherine the Great.

CONSTRUCTION (SCALE 1:20)

Barrel Mount a convenient length (minimum 80 mm) of 20 mm diameter rod (1) well into the three-jaw chuck. Face off the end, centre drill and drill out the bore to a diameter of 6 mm for a depth of 10 mm. Remove the piece from the lathe, centre punch 32 mm from the muzzle and, holding it in a machine vice, drill a 3 mm diameter hole for the lug to a depth of 7 mm.

Remount the work in the chuck with approximately 70 mm projecting and the muzzle end supported on a revolving centre. Set the top-slide to an angle of 5° and taper-turn the barrel to the dimensions shown. Now reduce and shape the metal around the cascable, leaving approximately 3 mm in diameter securing the button to the parent metal in the chuck. Carefully hacksaw through this and file the button to a smooth curve. (Alternatively, the barrel can be turned between centres and reversed in position for forming the cascable and button. In this case, the chase should be protected with a band of copper to avoid damage from the lathe carrier.)

The barrel lug (9) is shaped from 6 mm square bar, or from off-cuts from the carriage sides. Hacksaw and file to 14 mm x 6 mm square. Centre punch 3 mm from one end, drill out the 3 mm trunnion hole and file the end to a semi-circular shape. Mount the piece in a four-jaw chuck, face the opposite end

and reduce to a diameter of 3 mm for a length of 6 mm. A 6 mm square flat, filed onto the barrel, will ensure a flush fit for the shoulder of the lug.

Carriage sides Using a card or sheet metal template, mark out the two sides (3) on 70 mm x 30 mm x 6 mm strips. Centre punch and drill out the six 3 mm rod/bolt holes in one of the sides and use this as a guide to drill out the second side. Now hacksaw off the waste metal and file each side to shape using a half-round file for the hollow curves. Finally, clamp both sides together in the vice and drawfile to ensure symmetry. During drilling and filing, short pins of 3 mm welding placed in the holes already drilled can be used to position the two sides accurately.

Axletree and tie bolts Saw off a 48 mm length of 6 mm for the axletree (6) and face off each end to a final length of 46 mm. Position in the chuck with 22 mm protruding and turn down to a diameter of 4 mm for a distance of 20 mm. Now reposition with a further 6 mm protruding and cut the central groove with a round-nosed tool. Finally, reverse in the chuck and reduce the other half to 4 mm in diameter for a distance of 20 mm.

The two tie bolts (7) are made from 20 mm x 6 mm diameter

32-PDR. CARRONADE

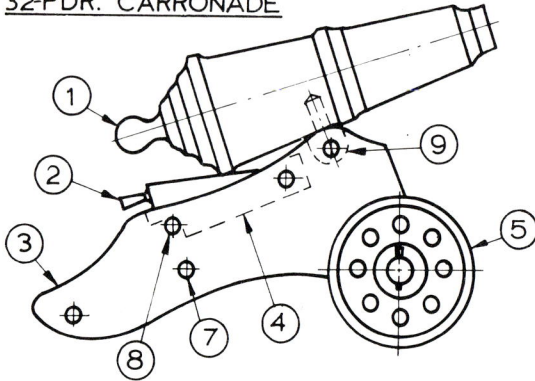

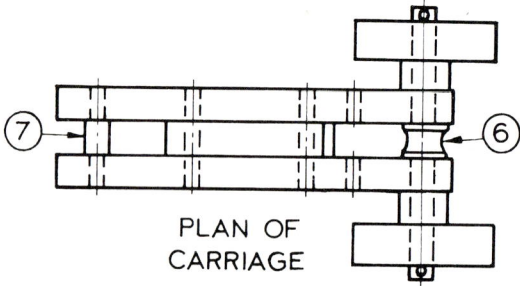

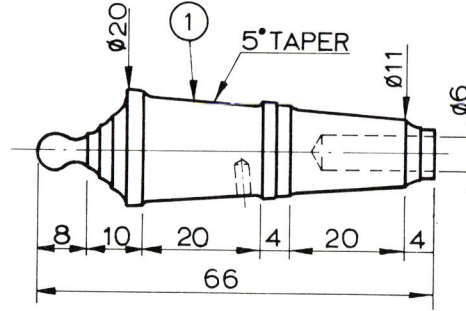

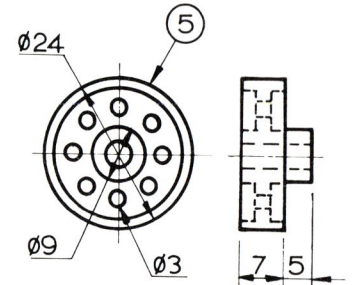

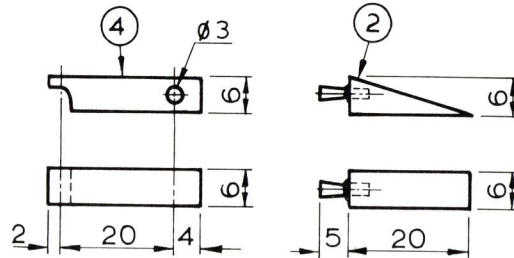

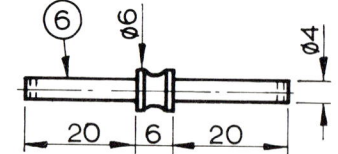

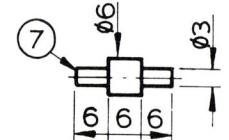

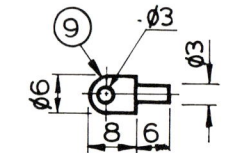

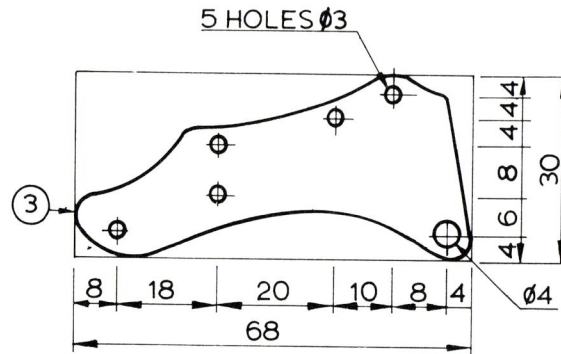

PLAN OF CARRIAGE

5° TAPER

Ø20 Ø11 Ø6

8 | 10 | 20 | 4 | 20 | 4

66

Ø24 Ø9 Ø3

7 | 5

5 HOLES Ø3

44 8 6 4

30

8 | 18 | 20 | 10 | 8 | 4

68

Ø4

Ø3

2 | 20 | 4

5 | 20

6

Ø6

20 | 6 | 20

Ø4

Ø6 Ø3

6 | 6 | 6

Ø3

18

Ø3

Ø6

8 | 6

ITEM	NAME	NO.	CUTTING SIZE
1	BARREL	1	20 DIA. ROD
2	WEDGE	1	21 x 6 x 6
3	SIDE	2	70 x 32 x 6
4	PLATFORM	1	27 x 6 x 6
5	WHEEL	2	25 DIA. ROD
6	AXLETREE	1	48 x 6 DIA. ROD
7	TIE BOLT	2	20 x 6 DIA. ROD
8	BOLT/TRUN.	3	20 x 3 DIA. ROD

SCALE 4:5

50

rods, faced off to a length of 18 mm and reduced to 3 mm in diameter.

Bolts   The two bed bolts and the barrel lug bolt are all cut from 3 mm diameter wire or welding rods (8) and faced off in the lathe to 18 mm in length.

Platform   The platform or bed (4) is made from a 27 mm length of 6 mm square bar, or a suitable off-cut from one of the carriage sides, filed to a length of 26 mm. Mark out, centre punch and drill the two 3 mm diameter holes 20 mm apart. Finish by hacksawing and filing out the step to the rear hole.

Wedge   A tapered off-cut from the carriage side can also be conveniently used to make the wedge or quoin (2). File to 20 mm long x 6 mm high and drill a 2 mm hole in the end to receive the small handle which is taper-turned from 3 mm diameter rod.

Wheels   Mount a convenient length of 25 mm diameter rod (5) in the three-jaw chuck with approximately 30 mm projecting. Face off the end, centre drill and drill out the 4 mm axle hole to a depth of 30 mm (i.e. sufficient for two wheels). Reduce the outside diameter to 24 mm for a length of 28 mm and further reduce to 9 mm in diameter for a length of 5 mm for the inner hub of the first wheel. The inner face of the wheel is now bored out to a depth of 2 mm between the hub and rim as shown on the drawing. Part off the wheel leaving a rim width of 7 mm.

Repeat these stages with the second wheel and then remount each in turn, gripping the inner hub in the chuck (preferably using a four-jaw for extra security), and carefully bore out to a depth of 2 mm between outer hub and rim for the outer face. Finally, using a template, mark out, centre punch and drill eight 3 mm diameter holes in each wheel.

Assembly   Lacquer the exposed faces of each part after polishing with emery cloth. Coat the barrel lug sparingly with epoxy resin and press it into the hole under the barrel. Now coat the tie rod and bolt ends with epoxy resin and assemble the carriage sides with the barrel, bed and axletree in position. Finally the wheels are held in position with two 1.6 mm diameter rivets or escution pins suitably cut to length. Alternatively, the axletree ends can be flared over with a hammer.

68-pounder carronade, circa 1805

At sea, carronades replaced many of the long cannon which could damage, but not sink, thickly clad men-of-war. The 68-pounder required only $5\frac{1}{2}$ lb of powder and was devastating at short range. This was dramatically proved by Captain Henry Trollope in the frigate *Glatton* who so surprised the French with his close-range fire power that he defeated a whole squadron of eight ships. At the crucial Battle of the Saints in 1782, the use of carronades gave an important advantage to Admiral Rodney's fleet in defending the British West Indian islands against the French under Admiral Comte de Grasse.

So popular did carronades prove that by 1791 over 400 Royal Naval vessels had been appropriately equipped, quite apart from extensive use of the smaller calibres by the merchant marine. Even on H.M. Bombs, four 68-pounders and six 18-pounders were substituted for the 13-inch mortar. Nelson himself saw the Battle of the Saints as a great tactical success, and, at Trafalgar in 1805, the first shot fired by Victory was from one of her two fo'c'sle 68-pounders, causing many casualties on the *Bucentaure*.

The smaller powder charge and backward thrust enabled the 68-pounder to be mounted via its lug on a wooden slide which recoiled on a slotted carriage. This could be traversed around a pivot pin or ranged with an elevating screw more quickly than the conventional design. Various permutations of sliding carriage and traversing platform were to evolve in the nineteenth century, both on land and sea. These included upwardly inclined slides for absorbing recoil and curved rails for the trucks to run in. Traditional 68-pounder ships' cannons, long 12-pounders and the two 68-pounder fo'c'sle carronades on their contrasting carriages can still be seen on H.M.S. *Victory*, preserved at Portsmouth to this day.

Eventually, armoured ships demanded high velocity shells fired from longer, more powerful guns. The problems of muzzle loading such guns in confined spaces encouraged the invention of breech loading mechanisms, while hydraulic buffers, and then hydro-pneumatic recoil systems, enabled more powerful propellants to be used. Consequently, carronades were not made after 1852, and this heralded the close of the era of smooth-bore muzzle-loaders which had spanned almost 600 years.

A few bronze guns were cast as late as 1870, remaining in service with the Indian Artillery until the end of the century. But composite barrels of shrunken steel tubes and high tensile wire provided far greater circumferential strength and were to be used in a new generation of guns, capable of reaching an unseen and unknown enemy many miles away.

Comparative sizes and performances of cannon and carronades

Name	Barrel length	Barrel weight	Normal charge	Range at 5°
Light 6-pounder cannon	4' 6"	5 cwt	$1\frac{1}{2}$ lb	1200 yards
Long 12-pounder cannon	9' 6"	34 cwt	4 lb	1800 yards
32-pounder carronade	4' 0"	17 cwt	2 lb 10 oz	1200 yards
32-pounder cannon	9' 6"	55 cwt	10 lb	2900 yards
68-pounder carronade	5' 2"	36 cwt	5 lb 10 oz	1400 yards
68-pounder cannon	9' 6"	87 cwt	22 lb	3000 yards

CONSTRUCTION (SCALE 1:20)

As in the original carronade, the carriage of the model may be made from hardwood or, as in the photograph on the previous page, from mild steel, and the instructions refer to the latter.

Barrel Mount a convenient length (minimum 120 mm) of 25 mm diameter rod (1) well into the three-jaw chuck. Face off the end, centre drill and drill out the bore to a diameter of 10 mm for a depth of 20 mm. Remove the piece from the lathe, centre punch 48 mm from the muzzle and, holding it in a machine vice, drill a 3 mm diameter hole for the lug to a depth of 7 mm.

Remount the piece in the chuck with approximately 105 mm protruding and the muzzle end supported on a revolving centre. Set the top-slide to an angle of 3° and taper-turn the barrel to the dimensions shown. Now reduce and shape the metal around the cascable, leaving approximately 4 mm in diameter securing the button to the parent metal in the chuck. Carefully hacksaw through this, file the end of the button to a smooth curve and file a flat on it, top and bottom. Finally centre punch, drill 2.5 mm and tap an M3 hole down through this for the elevating screw.

The barrel lug (2) is shaped from 8 mm square bar or an off-cut of the 8 mm strip used for the carriage. Hacksaw and file to size 16 mm x 8 mm square. Centre punch 4 mm from one end, drill out the 3 mm trunnion hole and file the end to a semi-circular shape. Mount in a four-jaw chuck, face the opposite end and reduce to a diameter of 3 mm for a length of 6 mm. An 8 mm square flat, filed onto the barrel, will ensure a flush fit for the shoulder of the lug. The trunnion (3) is made from 3 mm diameter rod, faced off to a length of 24 mm.

Slide Saw off a 65 mm length of 32 mm x 8 mm strip (6) and scribe a centre line around it using a surface gauge. From the mid-point on either face strike 32 mm radius arcs to each end and also mark out two holes 34 mm apart. Hacksaw off the waste corners and file the arcs to a smooth curve. Finally, centre punch,

drill out to a diameter of 2.5 mm, and tap the holes M3.

Carriage Saw off a 122 mm length of 40 mm x 8 mm strip (7) and reduce to an accurate length of 120 mm and a width of 38 mm either by careful filing or by milling. Scribe a centre line around it using the surface gauge, mark out a 25 mm radius arc at the front end with dividers and then hacksaw off the corners and file to a smooth curve. Mark out three 3 mm diameter holes and a 2.5 mm diameter hole along the centre line, centre punch and drill out. Now tap the 2.5 mm hole M3. Complete by cutting a 1 mm deep step over the pivot hole, either by milling, shaping or careful filing.

Experienced metalworkers may wish to cut a 65 mm x 3 mm slot down the centre of the carriage along which the slide can move back, as on the original carronades. This can be achieved by drilling and filing or, preferably, by milling.

Beds The carriage bed (8) is also made from 40 mm x 8 mm strip, but its full width is maintained. Therefore, hacksaw off a 46 mm length and file or mill accurately to 45 mm in length, then mark out and drill the 3 mm pivot pin hole 11 mm from the front edge.

Brackets These can be shaped from 22 mm lengths of 8 mm square bar (4) or from off-cuts of the 8 mm strip used for the slide or carriage. File square to a length of 20 mm, then mark out the contours on each side – an operation perhaps best performed with the aid of an aluminium or tinplate template. Mark out, centre punch and drill a 3 mm diameter trunnion hole. Finally saw away the waste metal, file the piece to shape and drill two 1 mm diameter holes for fixing onto the slide.

Elevating screw Mount a convenient length of 6 mm diameter rod (5) in the chuck with just enough protruding to parallel turn

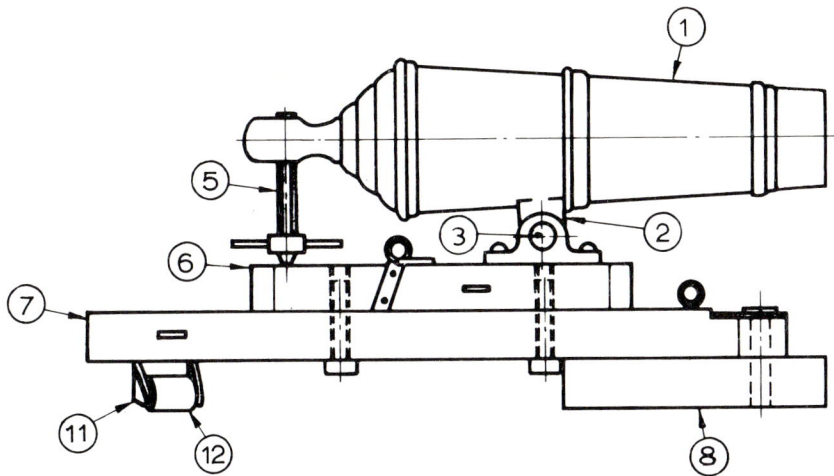

68-POUNDER SHIP MOUNTED
CARRONADE

SCALE 4:5

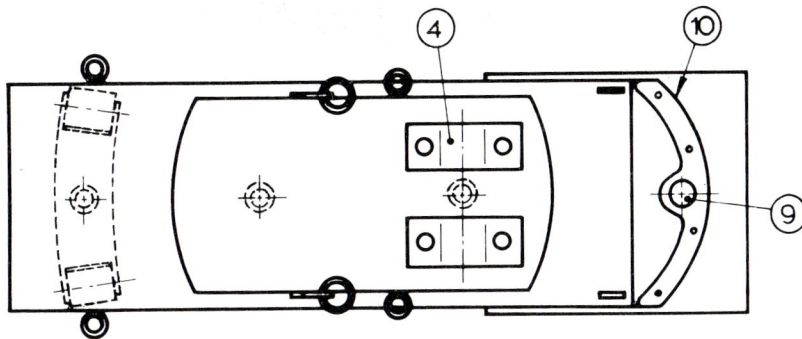

PLAN OF CARRIAGE

ITEM	NAME	NO.	CUTTING SIZE
1	BARREL	1	25 DIA. ROD
2	LUG	1	15x8x8
3	TRUNNION	1	26x3 DIA. ROD
4	BRACKET	2	22x8x8
5	SCREW	1	6 DIA. ROD
6	SLIDE	1	66x32x8 STRIP
7	CARRIAGE	1	122x40x8 STRIP
8	BED	1	46x40x8 STRIP
9	PIVOT PIN	1	6 DIA. ROD
10	PIVOT PLATE	1	40x15x1 SHEET
11	TRUCK BRACKET	1	12x40x8 STRIP
12	TRUCK	2	8 DIA. ROD

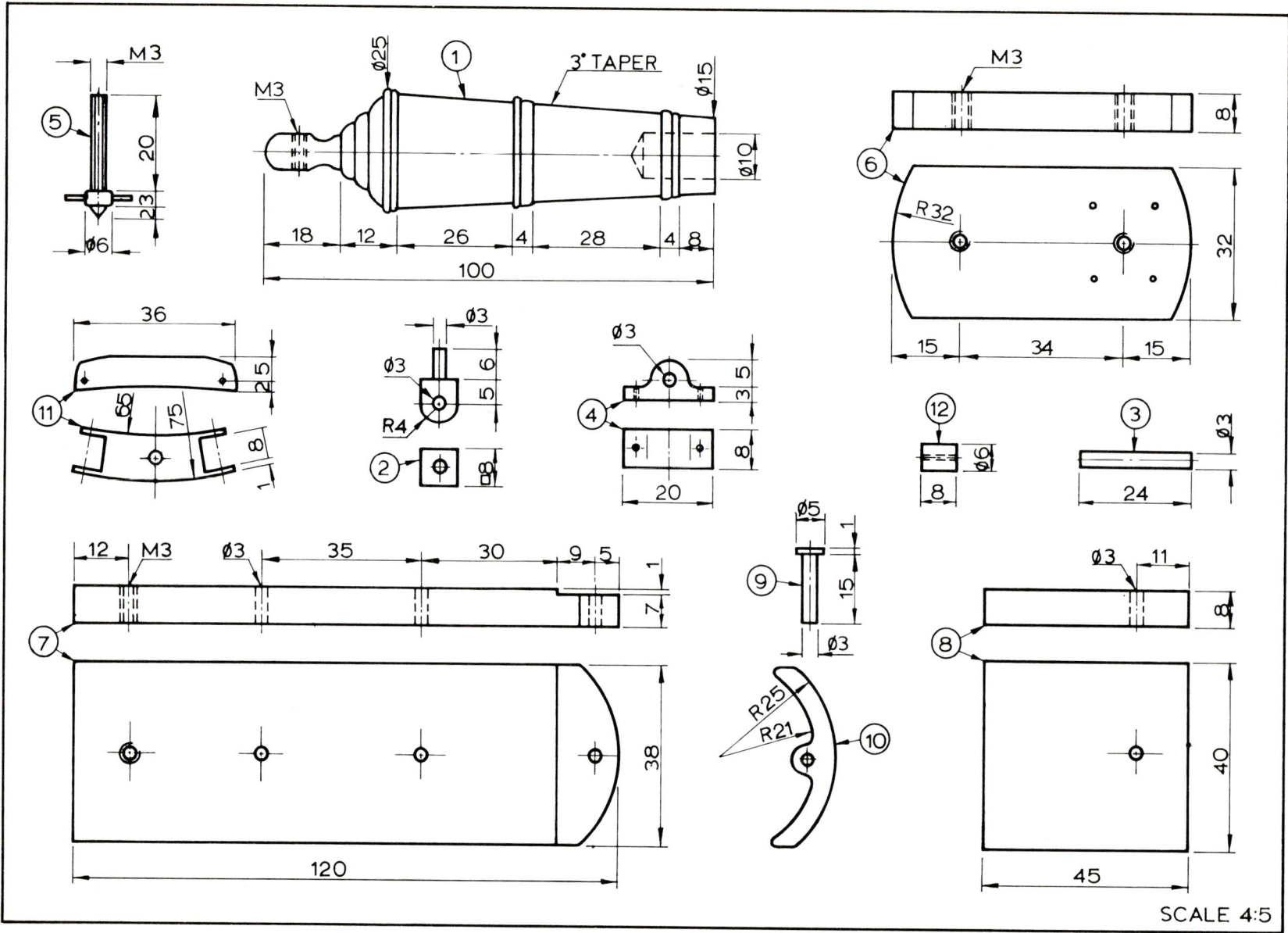

M3

⌀25

① 1

3° TAPER

⌀15

M3

⌀10

⑤ 5

20

23

⌀6

18   12   26   4   28   4 8

100

M3

⑥ 6

R32

32

15   34   15

36

② 5

⌀3

⌀3

⌀3

65

75

8

1

⑪ 11

Ø3

5
6
5

R4

② 2

8

④ 4

3
5

8

20

⑫ 12

⌀6

8

③ 3

⌀3

24

12   M3   Ø3   35   30   9 5

1

7

⑨ 9

⌀5
1

15

⌀3

⌀3   11

8

⑦ 7

R25
R21

⑩ 10

⑧ 8

38

40

120

45

SCALE 4:5

down to 3 mm in diameter for a length of 20 mm. If carried out carefully this may be achieved without resorting to use of the tailstock. Remove the metal from the lathe and hacksaw off 6 mm along from the shoulder and remount in the lathe so that the 2 mm conical point can be turned. Remove again from the lathe, file a small chamfer at the opposite end and cut the screw thread with an M3 die.

Truck bracket From the 40 mm x 8 mm strip, saw a piece 12 mm wide and mark out the 75 mm and 65 mm arcs using French curves. Alternatively, these can be marked out before sawing the piece off, using spring dividers. File the outer contours of the bracket to shape. Now carefully mark out a slot at either end for the trucks, remove most of the metal by drilling an 8 mm diameter hole, and complete by hacksawing and filing out the remainder. Holding the work at the correct angle in a machine vice, drill 1 mm diameter holes at either end for the truck axles. Finally drill and countersink the 3 mm hole.

The two trucks (12) are made from 8 mm diameter rod, faced off, drilled 1 mm, reduced to 6 mm diameter and parted off to a length of 8 mm in the lathe.

Pivot pin and plate The pin (9) is turned from 6 mm diameter rod, faced off and reduced to 5 mm diameter for 18 mm or so.

Then further reduce to 3 mm diameter for 15 mm and part off, leaving a flat head of 1 mm.

Cut the plate (10) from 1 mm sheet with a junior hacksaw, and carefully file to shape. Finally, drill a 3 mm diameter pivot hole and four small 1 mm diameter holes.

Assembly Polish each part with emery cloth and coat all exposed surfaces with lacquer. If a hardwood carriage has been made, finish with fine glass paper and polish with semi-matt polyurethane or wax.

Fix the barrel lug into position using epoxy resin. Position and fix the two trunnion brackets on the slide with cut-off panel pins and epoxy resin. The pivot plate is similarly positioned on the carriage front. An M3 screw plus a dab of epoxy resin should be used to hold the truck bracket in place at the rear of the carriage. Two lengths of pin, riveted or glued into place, will act as axles for the trucks.

Assemble the slide on the carriage with two M3 cheese or round head screws. Fix the carriage to its bed with the pivot pin. A touch of epoxy resin can be used to lock the pin in the bed. Finally, press the trunnion through the brackets and barrel lug, again using small amounts of adhesive to fix the parts in place, and screw the elevation screw into position. If breeching eyes are added, glue them into 1 mm diameter holes.

10-inch iron mortar, circa 1850

Until 1780, bronze was preferred for mortar barrels because of the difficulty of casting iron. Having been successfully adapted from the civilised practice of bell founding, bronze was also valued for its lightness, its elasticity allowing thinner walls. Although generally referred to as 'brass' the alloy was nine parts copper to one part tin and therefore more properly a bronze. But despite its toughness, bronze was susceptible to wear, thereby increasing windage. The vent also became enlarged and needed 'bouching' with a copper insert to withstand the effects of burning powder. During the Peninsular War the heat of intensive firing softened bronze barrels so much that they drooped, and from 1811 onwards iron gained in popularity, particularly as manufacturing techniques improved.

The 10-inch iron mortar was one of the later designs, dating from the middle of the nineteenth century. It had significantly thicker walls, and weighed half as much again as its brass equivalent. The barrel was of a rationalised design with the reinforce much reduced, and it incorporated a conical 'Gomer' chamber into which the shell wedged. This exploited to the maximum the initial thrust of explosion. Consequently, the effective range was doubled to 2500 yards. Like the barrel, the bed was made of cast iron. The sides were connected by tie bolts and transoms (omitted from this model). Capstans were retained for extra leverage dur-

ing levelling or traversing: laborious tasks, for a plumb-line had first to be aligned on target and the mortar slowly orientated until a chalk line along its barrel coincided with the plumb-line.

Unlike most other guns, mortars were only rarely fitted with wheels, heavy barrel and bed being transported ready-assembled on a four-wheeled sling waggon, while smaller mortars and their beds were transported separately on lighter two-wheeled sling carts. However, by the middle of the nineteenth century, a bed was designed to include a short trail and an axletree on to which wheels could be mounted. One weapon which did combine the lightness and mobility of the field gun with the ability to lob a large projectile was the howitzer, which was, in effect, a small mortar on wheels, capable of firing at the enemy, high over the heads of one's own troops. This was demonstrated at Waterloo when six howitzers cleared Hougoumont Wood of the French within ten minutes, missing the British completely.

Because mortar barrels could not be rifled to advantage (since their projectiles flew on curved rather than 'straight' projectories) these mortars were the last of the smooth-bore, muzzle loading guns. Today, although the term 'cannon' is obsolete, except when applied to some small calibre weapons such as those used in aircraft, 'mortars' and 'howitzers' are still very much with us in their contemporary forms.

Comparative sizes and performance of the mortars

Bore	Material	Task	Barrel length	Barrel weight	Shell weight	Maximum range
8″	Brass	Land Service	2′ 1¼″	4¼ cwt	46 lb	1600 yards
10″	Iron	Land Service	2′ 9″	16 cwt	93 lb	2500 yards
13″	Brass	Land Service	3′ 7½″	25 cwt	200 lb	1300 yards
13″	Brass	Sea Service	5′ 3″	82 cwt	200 lb	4100 yards

10" IRON MORTAR

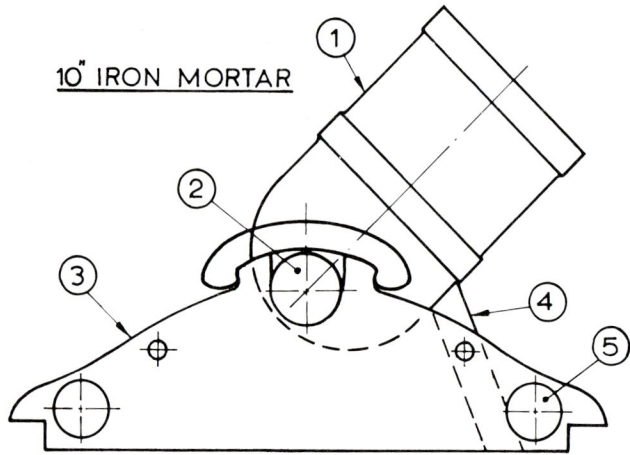

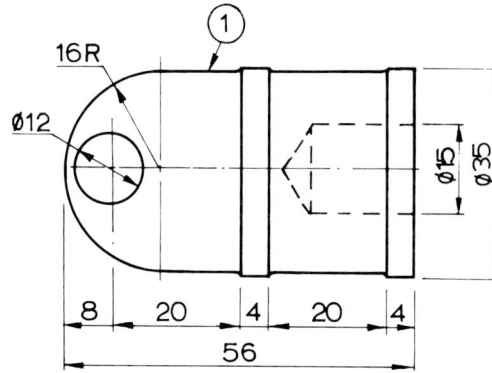

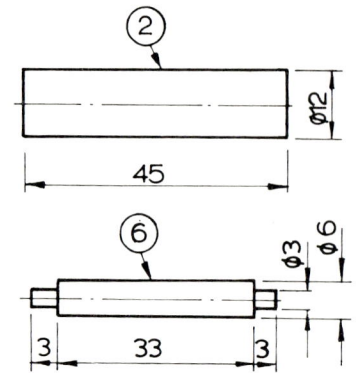

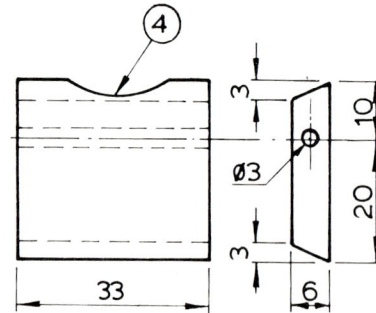

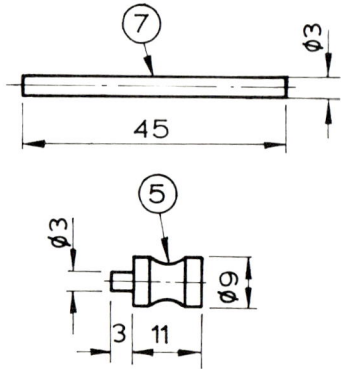

PLAN OF CARRIAGE

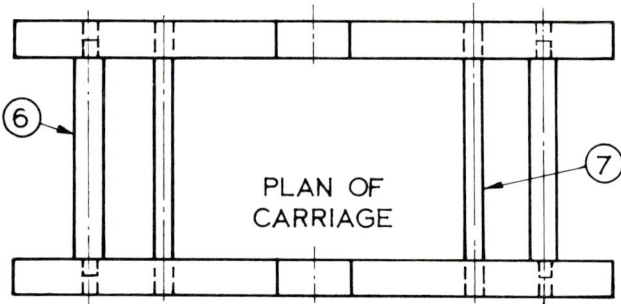

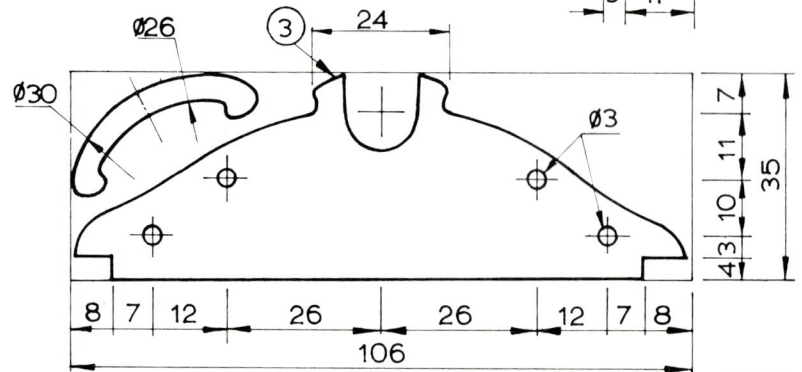

16R
Ø12
Ø15
Ø35
8 20 4 20 4
56

2
Ø12
45

6
Ø3 Ø6
3 33 3

7
Ø3
45

4
3
Ø3
3
10
20
33 6

5
Ø3
Ø9
3 11

Ø26
Ø30
3 24
Ø3
7
11
10
35
3 4
8 7 12 26 26 12 7 8
106

ITEM	NAME	NO.	CUTTING SIZE
1	BARREL	1	36 DIA. ROD
2	TRUNNION	1	46 x 12 DIA. ROD
3	SIDE	2	108 x 40 x 6 STRIP
4	BARREL REST	1	35 x 32 x 6 STRIP
5	CAPSTAN	4	10 DIA. ROD
6	TIE ROD	2	40 x 6 DIA. ROD
7	TIE ROD	2	46 x 3 DIA. ROD

SCALE 4:5

CONSTRUCTION (SCALE 1:20)

Barrel Saw off a 60 mm length of 36 mm diameter rod (1) and mount in the three-jaw chuck. Face off the end, centre drill, pilot drill and drill out the bore of the barrel to a diameter of 17 mm and a depth of 30 mm. Reverse in the chuck and face off the breech end to give an overall length of 56 mm. Use the lathe tool to scribe a centre-line down each side of the barrel and centre punch 8 mm from the breech end. Now hold in a machine vice and drill out a 12 mm hole for the trunnion.

Return the piece to the chuck, gripping approximately 12 mm and supporting the muzzle end on a revolving centre. Parallel turn to a diameter of 35 mm to within 3 mm of the chuck, then reduce to a diameter of 32 mm between the reinforcing rings. Finally, wrap a protective copper sleeve around the rings, remount the barrel in the chuck with the breech end outwards and turn a 16 mm radius curve, taking particular care around the trunnion hole. The trunnion itself (2) is made from 12 mm diameter rod, faced off to a length of 45 mm.

Carriage sides Mark out the sides (3) on 108 mm x 40 mm x 6 mm strips, using a card or sheet metal template. Centre punch and drill out the four 3 mm tie rod holes and the 12 mm trunnion hole in one of the sides. Use this as a guide to drill out the second side. At this stage the two capsquares may be marked out on the waste metal.

Next, by a combination of drilling, chiselling and hacksawing, remove the waste metal and file the sides and capsquares to shape. Finally, clamp the two sides together in the vice and drawfile to ensure symmetry. During the drilling and shaping operation, short pins of 3 mm rod should be placed in the 3 mm holes to position the two sides accurately.

Tie rods The large rods (6) are made from two 40 mm lengths of 6 mm diameter rod. Face off one end of the first axle and turn down to 3 mm in diameter for a length of 3 mm. Mark 33 mm from this shoulder and face off and reduce the opposite end to 3 mm in diameter up to the mark. Now repeat with the second axle, ensuring that both are identical lengths.

The small rods (7) are cut from 3 mm wire or welding rods, faced off to 45 mm in length.

Capstans Mount a length of 10 mm diameter rod (5) in the lathe with approximately 20 mm protruding. Face off the end and parallel turn to a diameter of 9 mm, then further reduce to 3 mm in diameter for a length of 3 mm. Now cut the groove with a round-nosed tool and part off the first capstan to an overall length of 14 mm. Alternatively, hacksaw it off, and remount in the lathe to face off the cut surface. Repeat these operations for the remaining three capstans.

Barrel rest Saw off a 35 mm length of 30 mm x 6 mm strip (4) and file square to a length of 33 mm. Mark out the bevels and the position of the 3 mm hole using a surface gauge or spring dividers. Centre punch and drill the hole, file the bevels and complete by filing a concave curve to fit the barrel.

Assembly Polish each part with emery cloth and lacquer the exposed surfaces. Slot one small rod through the hole in the barrel rest; coat the rod ends sparingly with epoxy resin and assemble the carriage. When the resin is set, glue the capstans in place. Finally glue the trunnion into the barrel, place the barrel on the carriage and glue the capsquare in position. Alternatively the capsquares may be locked into position using pins, as has been done in the photographed model (page 58).

CONVERSION TABLES

To convert inches to millimetres multiply by 25.4

A convenient approximation is that 1 inch = 25 mm

A useful close approximation is that $1/16'' = \dfrac{60''}{1000} = 16$ SWG $= 1.6$ mm

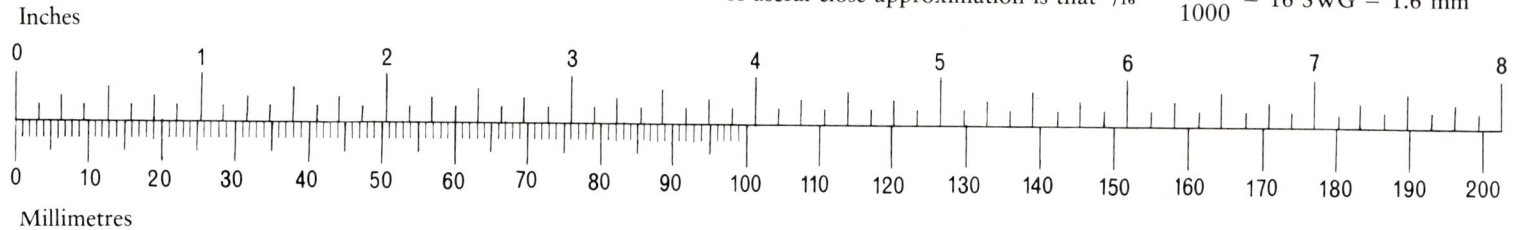

Inches

Millimetres

mm	inches
1	0.0394
5	0.197
10	0.394
15	0.591
20	0.787
25	0.984
30	1.181
35	1.378
40	1.575
45	1.772
50	1.969
55	2.165
60	2.362
65	2.559
70	2.756
75	2.953
80	3.150
85	3.346
90	3.543
95	3.740
100	3.937

Inch Fractions	Inch Decimals	mm
$1/64$	0.01562	.397
$1/32$	0.03125	.794
$3/64$	0.04687	1.191
$1/16$	0.0625	1.588
$5/64$	0.07812	1.984
$3/32$	0.09375	2.381
$7/64$	0.10937	2.778
$1/8$	0.1250	3.175
$9/64$	0.14062	3.572
$5/32$	0.15625	3.969
$11/64$	0.17187	4.366
$3/16$	0.1875	4.736
$13/64$	0.20312	5.159
$7/32$	0.21875	5.556
$15/64$	0.23437	5.953
$1/4$	0.2500	6.350
$17/64$	0.26562	6.747
$9/32$	0.28125	7.144
$19/16$	0.29687	7.541
$5/16$	0.3125	7.938
$21/64$	0.32812	8.334
$11/32$	0.34375	8.731
$23/64$	0.35937	9.128
$3/8$	0.3750	9.525
$25/64$	0.39062	9.922

Inch Fractions	Inch Decimals	mm
$13/32$	0.40625	10.319
$27/64$	0.42187	10.716
$7/16$	0.4375	11.113
$29/64$	0.45312	11.509
$15/32$	0.46875	11.906
$31/64$	0.48437	12.303
$1/2$	0.5	12.700
$33/64$	0.51562	13.097
$17/32$	0.53125	13.494
$35/64$	0.54687	13.891
$9/16$	0.5625	14.288
$37/64$	0.57812	14.684
$19/32$	0.59375	15.081
$39/64$	0.60937	15.487
$5/8$	0.625	15.875
$41/64$	0.64062	16.272
$21/32$	0.65625	16.669
$43/64$	0.67187	17.066
$11/16$	0.6875	17.463
$45/64$	0.70312	17.859
$23/32$	0.71875	18.256
$47/64$	0.73437	18.653
$3/4$	0.75	19.050
$49/64$	0.76562	19.447
$25/32$	0.78125	19.844

Inch Fractions	Inch Decimals	mm
51/64	0.79687	20.241
13/16	0.8125	20.638
53/64	0.82812	21.034
27/32	0.84375	21.431
55/64	0.85937	21.828
7/8	0.875	22.225
57/64	0.89062	22.622
29/32	0.90625	23.019
59/64	0.92187	23.416
15/16	0.9375	23.813
61/64	0.95312	24.209
31/32	0.96875	24.606
63/64	0.98437	25.003
1	1.000	25.400
1 1/8	—	29
1 1/4	—	32
1 3/8	—	35
1 1/2	—	38
1 5/8	—	41
1 3/4	—	45
1 7/8	—	48
2	—	51
2 1/4	—	57
2 1/2	—	64
2 3/4	—	70
3	—	76
3 1/4	—	83
3 1/2	—	89
3 3/4	—	95
4	—	101
4 1/4	—	108
4 1/2	—	114
4 3/4	—	121
5	—	127
5 1/4	—	133
5 1/2	—	140
5 3/4	—	146
6	—	152
12	—	305

CUTTING SPEEDS

Cutting speeds are the peripheral speeds of the work being turned in the lathe and vary according to its diameter and hardness.

Recommended peripheral speeds are:

Mild steel   24–30 metres per minute,
80–100 feet per minute

Brass   45–120 metres per minute,
150–400 feet per minute

Figures are for high speed steel tools and should be reduced by approximately one third for carbon steel.

Dia. of work (mm)	24m/min	30m/min	45m/min
2	3880	4850	7330
3	2590	3230	4580
4	1940	2420	3660
5	1550	1940	2800
6	1290	1610	2400
8	970	1210	1800
10	770	970	1500
12	640	810	1140
16	485	600	900
20	390	485	700
25	310	390	560

SUPPLIERS OF TOOLS, MACHINES AND MATERIALS

Boxford Machine Tools Ltd.
Wheatley,
Halifax HX3 5AF — Lathes

W. Canning & Co. Ltd.
Great Hampton Street,
Birmingham B18 6AS — Lacquers and polishing equipment

Cowell Engineering Ltd.
Rackheath,
Norwich NR13 6LF — Small lathes

Clarksons of York
53–57 Mayerthorpe
York YO3 7XB — Model engineering suppliers

Denford Machine Tools Ltd.
Victoria Works,
Brighouse,
Yorkshire HD6 1NB — Lathes

Elliott Machine Equipment Ltd.
BEC House,
Victoria House,
London NW10 6NY — Small lathes including the Emco Unimat

Gregory & Sutcliffe Ltd.
St. John's Road & Green Street,
Huddersfield HD1 5AS — Tools, ferrous and non-ferrous metals

John Hall Tools Ltd.
23 Churchill Way,
Cardiff CF1 4UE — Tools and machines

Heward & Dean Ltd.
90/94 West Green Road,
Tottenham,
London N15 4SR — Tools, machines, ferrous and non-ferrous metals and fittings

Macready's Metal Co. Ltd.
Usaspead Corner,
Pentonville Road,
London N1 9NE — Ferrous metals

Myford Ltd.
Beeston,
Nottingham NG9 1ER — Small lathes including ML10 and Series 7

A. J. Reeves & Co. Ltd.
Holly Lane,
Marston Green,
Birmingham B37 7AW — Model engineering suppliers

IMI Righton Ltd.
Brookville Road,
Witton,
Birmingham B6 7EY — Non-ferrous metals and fittings

C. Roberts & Co. (Steel) Ltd.
The Ickles,
Rotherham,
Yorkshire S60 1DP — Ferrous metals

J. Smith & Sons (Clerkenwell) Ltd.
42/54 St. John's Square,
London EC1P 1ER — Non-ferrous metals

K. R. Whiston Ltd.
New Mills,
Stockport SK12 4PT — Small tools, short lengths of ferrous and non-ferrous metals, and fittings